In the name of Allah
The Most Compassionate
The Most Merciful

Note for Librarians: A cataloguing record for this book is available from Library and Archives
Canada at www.collectionscanada.ca/amicus/index-e.html
ISBN 1-4251-1492-x

King Fahd National Library
Deposit number: 1425/5698 on 2004/10/11
ISSBN: 9960-46-653-1

*Printed in Victoria, BC, Canada. Printed on paper with minimum 30% recycled fibre. Trafford's print shop runs
on "green energy" from solar, wind and other environmentally-friendly power sources.*

TRAFFORD
PUBLISHING™

Offices in Canada, USA, Ireland and UK

Book sales for North America and International:
Trafford Publishing, 6E–2333 Government St.,
Victoria, BC V8T 4P4 CANADA
phone 250 383 6864 (toll-free 1 888 232 4444)
fax 250 383 6804; email to orders@trafford.com
Book sales in Europe:
Trafford Publishing (UK) Limited, 9 Park End Street, 2nd Floor
Oxford, UK OX1 1HH UNITED KINGDOM
phone +44 (0)1865 722 113 (local rate 0845 230 9601)
facsimile +44 (0)1865 722 868; info.uk@trafford.com
Order online at:
trafford.com/06-3251

10 9 8 7 6 5

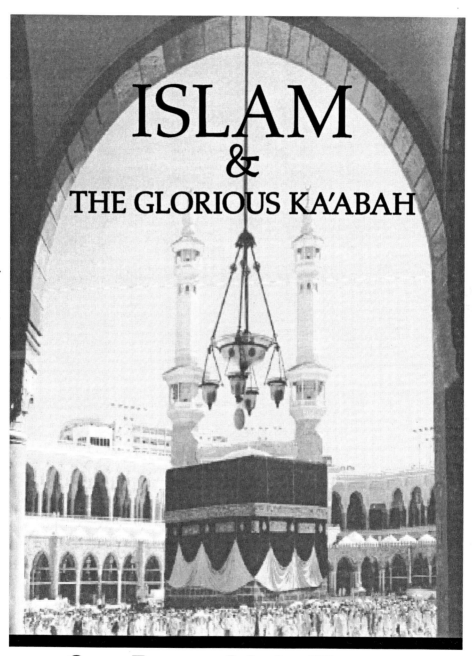

ISLAM
&
THE GLORIOUS KA'ABAH

SYED FAROUQ M. AL-HUSEINI

TABLE OF CONTENTS

Subject   **Pages**

*In the name of Allah The Most Compassionate
The Most Merciful*

FOREWORD

By the Grace of Allah the Merciful, and after saying the Salat and Salaam to Prophet *Mohammad* (Peace be upon him).

The ignorance about the most sacred and Glorified symbol or monument of Islam, gave me the urge to explain its beginning and emergence unto the world in a simple way and language, that along with scholars every one else would understand.

When I thought to write a booklet answering to the first question raised in this book "does God live here", things started coming down that I did not imagine. It was the end of the month of Ramadan and the beginning of the Haj months. There started coming new articles in our daily newspapers about the Ka'abah. The present day audio Video and TV system also was beneficial in hearing, seeing and listening to the scholars who would shed light on this subject. It all came in good time to help me in making this booklet into a book. I looked into my small library of books to find any books about the Kaabah. Fortunately there were also few old and valuable books I found, besides the books I newly obtained.

There are many books about the Ka'abah which are full of illustrated pictures came in the last few years. It supplied many useful information. I hope this book would be useful and beneficial in giving information being asked by people and helps in obtaining the knowledge about its subject.

This book is basically and essentially dedicated to the subject of The Ka'abah and Islam, which are interrelated. The Ka'abah is revered by Muslims as the symbol of the Oneness of God and towards which Muslims from all over the world face when offering their prayer rituals, in a uniform way.

I hope, this book will shed the light and brings the knowledge about Islam and its human and monumental symbols to its readers, and will open a door of understanding to this great religion.

To understand any subject, especially the religion, and to find the required knowledge correctly and without prejudice we should also have an open mind and heart while reading it. And I pray that it will enter the heart and minds with the necessary knowledge there in this book.

When we talk or write about any faith and religion we have also to know about its believers and followers. In every faith and religion there are the nice, pious and peaceful followers of the religion. Those are the well learned people and scholars who have sufficient knowledge of their religions or faiths, or who were brought-up and taught by those nice and pious and learned and peaceful people who could be their relatives, teachers or mentors in the society they live in. These people are an asset and are liked and welcomed every where.

But there are also the extremists, fundamentalists and selfish people in every religion and society who believe themselves to be the guardians or the sole keepers of those religions, and who misunderstand its concept or misinterpret its rules and principles according to their own restricted mind or limited understandings, and narrow vision. This is because of their meager knowledge about their own religion and faith. And they are not well-learned or properly educated people. They are the liabilities in each and every society. They may knowingly or unknowingly bring problems to themselves and their surroundings, and make people misunderstand their own religion and hurt it and hurt its cause and other believers in it through their rigid or false beliefs, harsh and irresponsible attitude, and wrong or narrow view of things. These are the worst type of people in any religion and faith, and they create hatred and animosity against the others even without any cause or valid or pertinent reasons.

This book is to make the reader understand Islam in its true form and without the prejudice against it and its disciples or followers. To give a wrong information in a book is worst than omitting that information. I was keen to include all the information I could obtain correctly. I have checked again and again what I have written, and have corrected some information from the last edition about the ardent enemies of the Prophet (peace be upon him), and added some more. I hope that this book will come to the expectation of its readers and hope that it will enlighten them correctly about its subjects.

This is the third edition, and I am grateful to who ever helped and contributed in the corrections compilation and completion of this book.

THIRD EDITION

This is the third edition for this book. Before publishing it I went back to the previous edition to edit and correct what I may find in typing or grammatical errors, which I was expecting to be minor or minimum.

What I have found which had to be corrected was far more than what I was looking for or expected. I had to re arrange paragraphs besides the usual printing errors.

It was like when some one would like to do a paint job in the house. He would be surprised to find the many dents and holes in the walls and the corners which had to be repaired and filled. Then he finds the plumbing and wiring systems also needs to be changed, and the faucets and the sockets need to be replaced because it was old or rusty. Then he finds that a room or two had to be expanded (or reduced in size) And for the sake of betterment of the house new balconies had to be added and some more engraving on the outside to change the face of the house. And at last the paint job is done and here you find a new book totally changed inside-out with a new and fine out look. I hope this new edition with its editing – corrections additions and omissions will be more beneficial and useful to the readers, and will helps more in understanding the subject in the book more easily and it will be helpful in bringing more knowledge to the readers, of its subject.

I hope that it will be looked into as a useful and important guide to the substance of Islam and pray Allah to accept this as a work of an individual who believes in Him and His oneness and believes in *Mohammad* (Peace be upon him) as His Messenger.

CHAPTER
1

THE GLORIOUS KA'ABAH

HOUSE OF GOD:

There is this cubic shaped monument draped in black which we see in the middle of the great mosque (Al Haram) in Makkah, and around which there are tens, hundreds or thousands of people going around it throughout the year according to the time of the day - morning, noon, afternoon, evening, night, mid-night, before dawn and at dawn and so on, twenty four hours a day people are going around this glorious cubicle. And as their numbers differs according to the times of the day, it also differs and varies a lot during the times of the year and according to seasons. Not the seasons as people of the world knows it. It is not the cold season or hot scason, it is not the summer or winter season, it is not the fall or spring seasons. These are the religious seasons, or occasions in Islam. Like the three months of Rajab, Sha'aban and Ramadan, which are the peak seasons for the Omra (small Hajj), or the two months of Dhu-Al-Qa'dah and Dhu Al Hijjah when it is the period for the Hajj or Great Pilgrimage. It has nothing to do with weather, like when it is raining, which is meager or very little during the year, or when it is sunshine which is 360 days of the year in the Arabian peninsula. And it is mostly hot or very hot during most time of the year in Makkah. This small cubical building which is shrouded in black, is very great in its value to the Muslims, and regarded as the most sacred monument. It is called the Kaabah and also known as the House of Allah or house of God. (Allah in Arabic language means God).

DOES GOD LIVE HERE?!

I have a friend from Asia, he used to work and live here in Saudi Arabia for many years, so he was fortunate enough to come to and visit Makkah many times during his stay here. He told me that in one of his visits to the Haram or the Grand Mosque in Makkah, and while he was sitting in front of the Ka'abah facing its door, watching and observing the pilgrims going around it, an old man from his country came and sat beside him and naively asked him, "Brother , does God live here, in this house?" pointing towards the Ka'abah.

This is an example of how people can be naïve or ignorant even in their own religion. They do not even think to ask themselves how God who created the universe and every thing in it would live in this small place!!! God is not an idol or deity or statue we build and put inside a place. God is Great, and He is far greater from this understanding and comprehension. He is the creator and we are His creatures. And He cannot be bound and limited in this place or in any other place. This ignorance about the most Sacred, Glorified and revered symbol and monument of Islam, gave me the urge to explain its beginning and emergence unto the world in a simple way and language, that along with scholars, every one else would understand. I am sure there are millions of people who are curious to know what is the Ka'abah, why it is called The House of God, why and when it was built, who built it, and what is inside it, and what it is built for, and so many other questions.

WHERE TO FIND GOD?

There is nothing which could be compared to God. To start with, no one has seen God, so that we can say where He might be in a definitive space or place. God is with us through His hearing and sighting and knowledge of every thing we say and do or even think about.

God lives in our hearts and in our minds and soul. He is every where we can see, and every where our sight can reach, or cannot reach. He is everywhere and nothing can encompass Him. He is not limited to any place. He is limitless. He is The Greatest. No one can define God. Because no one could see or imagine how He may look like. But we all know that He does exist, and He is on His throne in Heavens.

How did we know God does Exist?

He gave us humans the mind to think, and through it we know, that God does exist. If we think about all the things mentioned above, and if we look around us we would know that all these things did not become by itself (or like some people who would refer to it as created by "nature" - what nature? they should ask themselves.) God has created us all and every thing else.

Also we know for sure of God's existence through the Prophets and Messengers whom He choose to send to us all humans. Among the many great Messengers and Prophets, He has chosen and sent are; Noah, Abraham, Moses, Jesus, and the last one *Mohammad* (peace be upon all of them), to tell us about God and to teach us human beings how to worship Him.

Why House of God:?

The question some people may ask, why did ALLAH (God) wanted a House to be built for Him.

The Ka'abah is not built for God to be where He would be. It is the first house ever built on this planet and a place for us to be united around, and to pray, worship and remember Him all the time in a uniform way facing this house which symbolizes His Oneness. God has created us all to worship Him, and to build the world we are living in, as God mentions in the Qur'an:

And I have but created the Jinn and Human (only) to worship Me. (51:56)

The place where this House, the Ka'abah is built was choosen since the existence of this world, and long before humans came into being. In the belief of Muslims, the place where The Ka'abah was built, is the center of this world and the universe.

In all parts of this world, people built thousands of houses of God.

It is in the form of temples, Churches, and Mosques that are built to worship God in it. Unlike other places of worship there is the most important and common ground between this house The Ka'abah, and all the Muslim Mosques around the world:

1.   There is the unity of belief in the oneness of God. There are no deities, idols or statues erected or placed and worshipped or glorified in these houses of worship built in Islam, the mosques and The Ka'abah.

2.   All Mosques throughout the world are built to face towards the Ka'abah, or towards Makkah in which there is the Grand Mosque, and in the Grand Mosque is the Ka'abah. The direction it faces towards the Ka'abah is called the Qiblah for the Muslims.

No matter wherever they are, from Tokyo to Timbuktu or from Washington to Zimbabwe or from Australia and New Zealand to Tashkent, Muslims bow down and worship God, facing towards the Kaabah in Makkah. This is the sign of unity of their belief and the uniformity of their prayers and worship.

CHAPTER
2

MAKKAH AND THE KA'ABAH

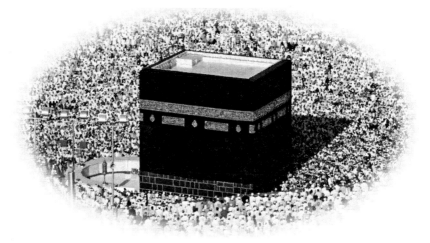

BRIEF HISTORY OF MAKKAH AND THE KA'ABAH:

The Ka'abah is the great monument of Islam which was originally re-built about four thousand years ago by the Messenger of Allah Prophet Ibrahim (Abraham) and his son Ismaeel (Ishmael), and Makkah is the city which was built around the Ka'abah since that long period and grew up to become one of the oldest cities of the world, and the most sacred city in Islam.

Messenger of Allah, Prophet Ibrahim, came from the north from Babil in Iraq and passing through Syria and Palestine came to this Place called Makkah or Bakkah in the ancient time. It was a valley near the passage where beduen tribes used to pass by during their travel. They would camp here and put-up tents to rest before continuing their journey. At that time it was a barren place, and was surrounded by hills and low mountains. There was nothing in it, and no-body was living there.

He brought with him his second wife Hajar and their baby son Ismaeel. He was going to leave them there. This was the will of God. From this barren place a new nation was to grow out of the heirs and descendents of Ibrahim and his son Ismaeel. From this nation there would shine throughout the world the light of Islam in the days to come, and which was revealed in history later on, as the Islamic religion which started from this region.

Prophet Ibrahim left his wife and child in this barren place alone and without anything with them, except for some food and little water. And when he was far away and out of their sight, and at the corner of a hill, he turned around and facing the direction of the place where he left his helpless wife and child, (and where eventually the Kaabah was going to be built later), Prophet Ibrahim pleaded and prayed to God." As mentioned in the Qur'an, thus:

Ibrahim said : 'Lord' make this *¹ a land of safety. Preserve me and my descendants from serving idols. Lord, many have they led astray. He that follows me shall become my brother, but if anyone turns against me, you are surely forgiving and merciful.

'Lord, I have settled some of my offspring in a barren valley near Your sacred House, so that they may Establish (Prayers) true worship. And so incline the hearts of some people to yearn towards them (like them with kindness), and provide them with the fruits (produce or bounty), so that they may give thanks.. 'Lord, You have knowledge of all that we hide and all that we reveal: nothing in heaven or earth is hidden from God. (Ibrahim:37) (*¹ Makkah).

STRIVING BETWEEN THE TWO HILLS:
{ ALSAFA AND ALMARWA}:

After the departure of Prophet Ibrahim, who had left, and seeing her-self and her baby son (Ismaeel) alone in this wilderness, his wife Hajar was anxious and afraid. Besides, the dates or the little food and water which was with them was going to finish. She didn't know what to do or expect. And in her bewilderment she hurried towards a near-by small hill called Alsafa. She climbed the hill and looked around and beyond to see if she can find any human being or sign of water. There was nothing. She then descended and ran towards another facing hill called AlMarwa, and climbed over it to look and find anyone beyond it on the other side of the hill. But nothing and no one was there either. So she hurried back towards the first hill in hope of finding some help coming. This way she went seven times back and forth between these two hills, The Alsafa and Al-Marwa. And all the time she was keeping sight of her child, where she left him. She had a feeling that help will come. Because she knew Prophet Ibrahim was commanded (inspired) by God to leave her, and her baby in this barren and wild place. And since it was God's will which prophet Ibrahim obeyed and carried out, she was confident that God will not leave them there without help. And so, after the seventh shuttle running or striving between the two hills and while she was on the Marwa hill, she saw the help coming in the form of a miracle, an angel was standing be her child.

The Miracle of ZAM ZAM Spring Water:

While she was on the "Marwa" hill she saw an Angel standing beside her baby child. And with his unnatural and divine power and force he dug on the ground, and there became a spring of water which started flowing beside the child. She ran down towards her child. In her happiness and excitement she started shouting "Zam Zam"-"Zam- Zam" or "Stop-Stop". She was afraid that this spring will over flow on land. But the spring was confined in its place. She was thankful to God for this great gift in this desert, and barren land. This spring-well was to become the cause for the building and growing of Makkah, as we will see how it did attract the Arabian tribes to come and settle besides it.

After the discovery or the presence of this spring well, she was again becoming worried and anxious as the day was passing by and darkness of the night was approaching and she and her baby were alone in this wilderness. God was kind, and in a short-while she was going to have the good company of a passing-by tribe, which would alleviate her anxiety and fear.

Jorham Tribe:

About this time, a Yemeni tribe called " Jorhm" was on its way from Yemen in the south traveling or migrating towards Syria and Palestine in the north. This tribe was passing near the place of Makkah, when they surprisingly noticed birds flying over the area. The leader and members of the tribe knew that these birds are an omen sign. They knew that birds fly and hover over areas where people and water are available. So they veered towards this place. And when they came close they found Hajar with her baby son Ismaeel besides this new found water spring. They were very happy to find water in this area, and asked her permission to put-up their camp there, beside them. She also was delighted to see these people in this wilderness, and she willingly agreed for and welcomed them to put their camp. She thanked God for granting her and her child this spring and sent them these people to be with in their safe company.

THE BEGINNING AND EVOLUTION OF THE CITY OF MAKKAH:

This was the start of the building of Makkah. God has willed this place where a new nation was to grow from this place. God has also granted the prayers of His Messenger Prophet Ibrahim, when he asked and prayed to God before he departed this area leaving his wife Hajr and their son. He had prayed, thus:

'Lord, I have settled some of my offspring in a barren valley near Your sacred House, so that they may Establish (Prayers) true worship. And so incline the hearts of some people to yearn towards them (like them with kindness), and provide them with the fruits (produce or bounty), so that they may give thanks.

'Lord, You have knowledge of all that we hide and all that we reveal: nothing in heaven or earth is hidden from God. (Ibrahim:37) .

After they decided to stay here this tribe started to build their houses or homes around the area. They built a house for Hajar and her son

Ismael, who started growing up among this "Jorham" tribe. Later on many more people and traveling caravans joined them and so Makkah started to grow up as a village and then a town, and in due time became a major city and central or main hub for people and caravans, criss crossing the Arabian Peninsula, especially between North and South and vice versa. It became a very important city, and became a pilgrimage and trade center, as time passes by. In due time Ismaeel also grew up to be a young man, and he married within this tribe.

Prophet Ibrahim visited Makkah several times as he was indeed in love with his son which he have left several years ago. His wife Hajr the mother of his son Ismaeel in the meantime died. Ismaeel married twice. He divorced his first wife after she ill-treated his father Prophet of Allah 'Ibrahim' when he came in one of his early visits to Makkah, while Ismaeel was away. (And later Ismaeel married again).

THE SACRED PLACE:

The place where the holy Ka'abah was built is a chosen place by God. It is designated for the purpose to Worship Him. Allah mentioned in the Qura'an The prayer of Prophet Ibrahim, thus:

'Lord, I have settled some of my offspring in a barren valley near Your sacred House, so that they may observe true worship.

So the sanctity of this designated or chosen place was already been made long before Prophet Ibrahim came and settled his family besides it, and later on built the Ka'abah or (The House of God) on it. It was so that people would remember God's presence when they pray towards this house, THE KA'ABAH. The place was designated and choosen by Allah since the existence of this world.

The Ka'abah originally was built by Adam father of humanity (peace be upon him) when he was descended from heaven on this planet. It was rebuilt by Prophet Ibrahim and his son Ismail (peace be upon them) on its foundation after it was wiped out and destroyed long time ago by the huge flood at the time of Noah (peace be upon him). And it is thus mentioned :

And as Ibrahim and Ismail raised the foundations of the house(while praying) **Our Lord accept from us (this service) Though Art The All Hearing All Knowing.** (2:127) The Cow.

The Ka'aba as built by Prophet Ibrahim

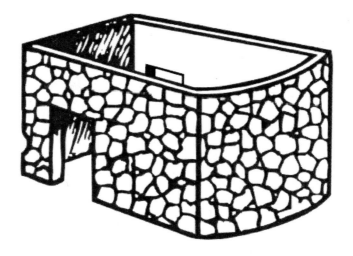

Artistic view of the Ka'aba built by Prophet Ibrahim (Abraham) and his son Ismaeel - about 4000 (four thousand) years ago.

THE BUILDING OF THE KA'ABAH:

In one of his visits to Makkah to see his son Ismael, Prophet Ibrahim was commanded to build a house or a building where people would pray and worship God. He was indicated the place where this building was to be erected or built. It was the same place where he left his wife and son on his first visit, and it is the place beside the Zam Zam spring. He told his son about this dream, and Ismaeel readily agreed to help his father. So Prophet Ibrahim and his son started to build the Ka'abah. Ismaeel carries and brings the bricks or stones and Prophet Ibrahim performs the construction and raises the building. During the construction Arch Angel Jebrael (Gabriel) brought them a white rectangular stone and indicated to make it in the corner of this house. The stone was white as marble, and it was a heavenly gift from God for this house.

After mission accomplished, and the house of prayer was completed and built, God commanded his messenger Prophet Ibrahim (Peace be upon him and upon all the Prophets) to call on people to come for Hajj, which he did, announcing this call in the valley. And it is mentioned in the Qur'an, Thus:

26. When we designated for Ibrahim the site of the Sacred Mosque We said: 'Worship none besides Me. Keep My House clean for those who walk around it, and those who stand upright or kneel in worship.'

27. Announce to all mankind to make the Hajj (pilgrimage). They will come to you on foot and on the backs of swift camels from every distant quarter;

28. They will come to avail themselves of many a benefit, and to pronounce on the appointed days the name of God over the cattle which He has given them for food. eat of their flesh, and feed the poor and the unfortunate.

29. Then let the pilgrims spruce themselves, make their

vows, and circle the Ancient House. Such is God's commandment. He that reveres the sacred rites of God shall fare better in the sight of His Lord. (Surat Al-Hajj - 26,27,28,29)

By the Grace of God this call and announcement to come for worship and Hajj spread and reached every where around the world, and since that time people started coming from every where to visit this house, and pray around it.

After completing the building of this house of prayer and worship, Prophet Ibrahim left Makkah and went back to where he came from. His son Ismaeel stayed in Makkah with his own family and children.

The Kaaba became the sacred house in the Arabian Peninsula. And people come to it from every where. They come to pray and worship God, and also do business among themselves. It became the envy of other people and tribes.

At the advent of Islam, this ritual was upheld, and the Muslims continued to visit it for Hajj or Omra (pilgrimage) to Makkah, after the Ka'abah was cleared and cleaned from idols and the deities which were in and around it, during the pagan era.

MAKKAH THE FAMOUS CITY:

In times to come many people and tribes came and settled in Makkah for three reasons. First: The spring water of Zam Zam, which flowed in there. Water was the most important, dear, precious and scarce commodity in that area. And finding this un-ending water supply nearby made them settle down in Makkah.

Secondly: The building of the Ka'aba in Makkah where people would pray to God, also made this city a famous one in the Arabian peninsula. Pilgrims would flock in from all over the Arabian Peninsula and it became a worship place.

Thirdly: It became a trading post or an economic and trade center for the people who would come from all over Arabia and far-away places bringing with them goods they would trade in or sell to each other in Makkah, and buy for themselves goods coming from different areas before they go back home. And thus Makkah started growing and flourishing through-out the history since the time of Prophet Ibrahim About 4000 (four thousand) years ago. It is the oldest populated city, where you will find all the earthly fruits which comes from all around the world and from every where, and all the year long. This is a true answer and acceptance of Prophet Ibrahim's prayers when he left his wife ad son, over there.:

Put in the hearts of men kindness towards them, and provide them with the earth's fruits, so that they may give thanks.

THE CHANGES:

With the popularity and growing fame of Makkah and the Ka'abah, it became the envy of tribes of other regions and places. People of different beliefs and religions also became envious. They found that people from all places were going to Makkah and not visiting their own towns or temples. This created hardship for their economy as well. So many tribes would invade Makkah. Some of them fared-well and settled there, and many were relapsed.

Later on and with the passing of time, some even brought their own statues and deities and erected it near the Ka'abah. In the wake of time the Jorham tribe became week in their religious beliefs, and eventually these idols or deities were being worshipped there instead of worshipping God Almighty. And the most famous among those deities or idols are the statues of Allat, Aloza, Manat and Hubal.

With the coming of Islam into Makkah in th 10th year of Hijri (620 AD), after the conquest of Makkah by Prophet *Mohammad* (Peasce be upon him), all these statues, idols or deities were destroyed and removed from within or around the Ka'abah. The Ka'abah became clean, and again took its place as the sacred House of God, and stayed so, and it become more honored and sanctified from that time.

THE FIRST ATTACK ON MAKKAH:

In the Northern part of the Arabian peninsula, there was the tug of war between the Roman Empire and the Persian Empire to get hold of, or rule the northern part of Arabia where Syria and Palestine and where the Ghassan tribes were the rulers. Some times the Romans win the area, and some times the Persians.

And seeing the popularity and hearing about the place of worship in Makkah where people would always go to, from the north and the south, the Romans thought that if they would sub-due the Arabs, and capture Makkah, they will permanently rule this area over the Persians. And after some strategic planning they thought if they would came from Yemen in the south they may not have a big resistance and would by surprise attack and take over Makkah easily, and so the people in the Arabian peninsula would come under their rule and influence. This way they will make it a permanent part of their empire, and win for good against the Persians Empire, who had some influence in the south, in Yemen.

But things did not go as well as they thought. Because, when they came by sea on the Yemani ports in the south, they found a strong resistance over land from the Arabian tribes who fought fiercely to stop the invaders, and the whole Roman army which was sent on this excursion was destroyed. And the Romans were defeated for good even before they have gone near Makkah.

THE ATTACK BY ELEPHANTS:

The Ethiopians also had an eye on the Arabian Peninsula. So they invaded Yemen in the south, and built a huge cathedral or temple there. It was most glittering sight as it was built without regards to expenses, and it was a fine piece of architecture. People were invited to visit this temple, but it did not have the attraction or the devotion like the house of God in Makkah even though the Kaabah was just a simple small rectangular building built with stones, rocks and clay.

This irritated the Governor and the General of the Ethiopian army named Abraha, who vowed that he will destroy the Ka'abah so that people will divert to his temple instead. He arranged a big and well equipped army under his command. He brought elephants from Africa for himself and his generals to ride on to Makkah to destroy the Kaabah. In the year 570 A.D this invading force arrived at Taif near Makkah, and camped over there. He was surprised he had not faced any real resistance so far.

When they camped near Makkah, his soldiers captured the live-stock or cattle they would find. And among these they took the cattles of Abdul Muttaleb the leader of Quraish, the most famous tribe in Makkah. He was the grand father of Prophet *Mohammad*, (who was born in that same year 570 AD) the same year the Ethiopians came on their elephants to attack the Kaabah.

Abraha heard about the young Abdul Muttalib, who was a famous and handsome leader of Quraish tribe, and he wanted to see him. When Abdul Muttalib heard about his cattle's confiscation, he went to see this Ethiopian General. When they met, he asked Abraha to release back the cattles which were taken by his army. Abraha was surprised and disappointed with this young man, who instead of discussing the major issue that he came for, which was to destroy the Kaabah or The House of God, this Quraish leader was interested in his cattles only. He told him so. To which Abdul Muttalib replied that "I am the lord (owner) of my cattle, and The House has its own Lord, who will defend it." Any way Abraha gave him back his cattles - and was about to find out how the Lord of The House would defend His House.

THE RETREAT AND DESTRUCTION OF THE ATTACKERS:

When time came for the offensive on the Ka'abah, strange things started happening. The elephants would not go to attack the Ka'abah, instead these animals would sit down and would not budge from their place whatever the soldiers would do, if directed towards Makkah. And whenever those animals were directed towards the opposite side or away from the Ka'abah they would willingly move. This made confusion in the Ethiopian army as they were not able to make these elephants move towards The Ka'abah in Makkah.

And later on another strange things started to happen. The sky became full of birds, flocks & flocks expressed as Aba-Beel in the Quran, which came hovering on top, and they started pelting the soldiers with small pebbles or stones they were carrying in their beaks and claws. And it was all a direct hit. And who-ever was hit with these stones were seriously injured and killed. Abraha and his army were wildly scattered and they retreated in haste towards Yemen in the south from where they came from, and he died miserably soon after he arrived there. And thus the Ka'abah or house of God was saved by its Lord.

And the Yemani people also got rid of the remaining forces and librated their country from this invading army. This incident is described in the Holy Quraan thus :

"In the Name of God, The Compassionate, The Merciful"

1. **Have you not considered how your lord dealt with the owner's of the Elephant?**

2. **Did He not make their plot go astray?**

3. **And He sent over them flocks of birds** (Ababeel)

4. **Pelting on them with stone of hard clay**

5. **And He made them like eaten straw.** – (Surah: Al-feil)

The Ka'abah and Maqam Ibrahim

The Ka'abah fully covered with the black coloured shroud, which is adorned with stripes and frames of verses from the Qur'an, embroidered in Gold.

In front of the Ka'abah is this small shrine where in the foot print of Prophet Ibrahim (Peace be upon him) preserved on the stone clay he used to stand on while building the Ka'abah.

The Ka'abah being wrapped with Kiswah

**The Ka'abah as it is seen now, before it is wrapped fully
and adorned with the Kiswa**

CHAPTER 3

RESTRUCTURE AND REBUILDING OF THE KA'ABAH

REBUILDING OF THE KA'ABAH:

In the long time since it was built about 4000 years ago, The Ka'abah has been rebuilt or renovated several times on the same foundations where it was originally been constructed. This was due to many factors including the aging of the building, the climatic factors and the floods. It was also been attacked and vandalized. The last time it was rebuilt before the advent of Islam was when *Mohammad* (peace be upon him) was a young man. And he was not yet proclaimed to become the last prophet and messenger of God.

All the tribes in Makkah were taking part in the rebuilding of the Ka'abah. Because they ran short of funds or "pure money", (money which is part of real income through trade and lawful deals and does not consist or contain income from gambling and drinks etc.) the Ka'abah this time was built short on its east and west sides, and so it became cubic shaped, instead of its original rectangular shape when built by Prophet Ibrahim and his son Ismael. The arc built on the south-east side does indicate the original area of the Ka'abah, and is part of the building originally built by Prphet Ibrahim. So the compulsory or obligatory prayers are not offered or performed within the arc area.

When they reached the point where they had to fix the exalted stone on the corner of the Ka'abah, all were hoping to be the ones who would have the honour to put this stone in its place. So they argued among themselves who or which tribe be the right one, or the fortunate one to have this honour. They were on the verge of fighting when some one suggested to wait for the first visitor who would enter the Ka'abah area. He would be the judge or arbiter, and he would decide this matter, and his decision would be binding to all. They all agreed to this suggestion.

At that time the young man, *Mohammad*, was the first one who entered the Ka'abah area. They all called with excitement, "Al Amin" came. (The trust worthy). They all trusted *Mohammad* for being the trust worthy and the truthful person they knew since his early days. So they called him and asked him to solved thier dilemma. *Mohammad* without hesitation asked them to have a Sheet of cloth, or a large robe they used to wear as their dress. He spread this cloth on the ground and placed the stone on it. He then asked that one person from each tribe would hold on to the cloth and raise it with the stone in it. This way all the tribes had the opportunity to share in this noble task. They raised the stone to the level where it was supposed to be placed, and he took it from there by himself and placed it in its place in the corner of the Ka'abah.

The Corner Stone

**These small pebbles are what is left of the Black Stone
in the corner of the Ka'abah**

WHAT IS THE CORNER STONE?:

When Prophet Ibrahim and his son Ismaeel were building the Ka'abah, The Angel Gabriel came with a big white stone. He told them it is God sent gift from heaven, and that they should place it on the corner of The Ka'abah. He indicated to them the east corner, and the place where it was to be placed.

From this corner the pilgrims start and end their seven rounds (circumambulation) around the Ka'abah. When Prophet of Islam *Mohammad* (peace be upon him) came during the Hajj He leaned into and kissed this stone. Thus Muslims also revere and kiss this stone, when they can, as their prophet did.

The black stone or the corner stone originally was white and big, rectangular (oblong) shaped. It was very white in colour, and which through the long time and ages that it was placed there became worn and its colour changed from white to dark, until it became black. According to people who saw it when the Qarametah leader vandalized it from its place. It was about 1 foot long, and was big enough to be made a corner stone.

During the ages, this stone has been vandalized, broken and its pieces stolen. The most incredible and wicked attack on the stone came from the Khawarej or Qarametahs who wanted it to be fixed in their temples in the eastern part of Arabia. It was vandalized about 1107 years ago in the year 317 (AH) / (935 AD) by the Qarametah who attacked the people in the Haram area and broke the stone from its place and took it with them where they built their own temple in the eastern part of Arabia, and erected it in there.

Its place in the Ka'abah in Makkah remained empty for about twenty two years, and after the death of this Qarametah leader the corner stone or whatever of its pieces left was brought back in the year 339 (AH) to Makkah, and was put back in its empty place.

It have since been attacked and vandalized many times, and broken into pieces. By now there are but eight (8) small pieces left in its place, the biggest of which is about the size of a Date.or an Olive

The other small pieces or fragments were mixed as paste and fixed around these remaining pieces inside the silver frame.

WHAT IS INSIDE THE KA'ABAH?:

As can be seen in the illustration the Ka'abah is empty inside except for the Three pillars. They were originally erected inside the Ka'abah by Abdullah Ibn Al Zubair who was the Governor or wali of Makkah at the Khilafat Al Rashedeen time, the companions and successors of the prophet *Mohammad* (peace be upon him) during the first century of Islam. He built the roof and erected these pillars so as to support the roof of the Kaabah. These pillars are made of the most strongest wood as it continued to support the roof of the Ka'abah for the last 1400 years. Originally when it was built by Prophet Abraham The Ka'abah had no roof on top of it.

The Kaabah was renovated at the time of King Fahad in 1999AD. / 1419 Hijra. The new pillars are of high quality wood chosen and brought from deep jungles in Asia. There are other roof supports made of wood too. This wood is processed and cut in Saudi Arabia in the wood factory near Makkah and installed inside the Ka'abah.

Whoever is fortunate to enter or visit inside the Ka'abah may offer voluntary prayers towards any side or direction from inside, as the Prophet of Islam (peace be upon him) did after clearing it from idols or deities when he entered Makkah victoriously on the 9th year after his migration from it. He offered two raka'ats towards each side thanking Allah for the victory of Islam.

Maquette inside view of the Ka'abah

The architectural maquette to show the Ka'abah from inside.
Except for the three pillars which supports its roof - The
Ka'abah is empty - no statues or relics or even a place to put
such things inside.

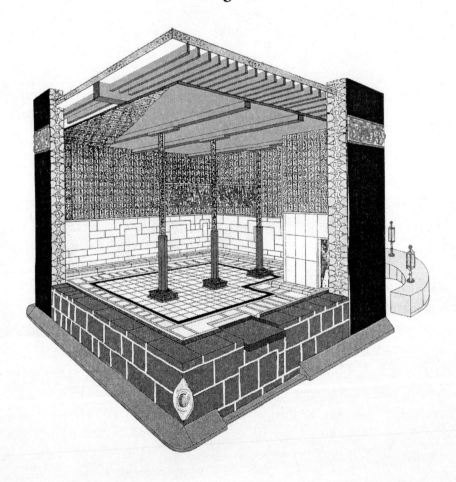

How big is the Kaabah:

The Ka'abah is a small building in size, but a very large and great perspective monument and holy place in Islam. It carries a significant moral, spitritural and religions values in to the hearts and minds of Muslims around the world.

It is a cubic shaped building, with an arc extention on its North-East side. Which was originally part of the main building built by Prophet Ibrahim, and was cut short when it was being rebuilt by Quraish. Its dimensions are as follows:

From the corner stone in the East to the Syrian corner (East to north) 11.68 meters, this side include the main and only entrance door. The corner of the black stone faces east, the other corners of the Kaabah faces the other three directions.

1. From the corner stone towards the Yemeni corner (East to the South) 10.18 meters

2. From the north corner to the west corner 9.90 meters.

3. From the Yemeni corner to the west 12.04 meters.

4. The height 12.95 meters.

THE DOOR:

The Kaabah entrance door is built high in its North Eastern wall. It is about 2.20 meters higher from the ground or the floor at the TAWAF area. The door itself is about 3.00 meters high and 2.00 meters wide, and it has two shutters in one frame. The door is built high above the ground for two reasons:

1.   In the old days rain water and floods used to fill the area around the Kaabah because it is in the lower valley, and this way the door itself stays high and rain and flood water would not enter inside the Kaabah.

2.   The door is not used casually, and is not opened daily, and it is opened only when it is necessary like when it is time to wash and clean the Kaabah, which is done by Governor of Makkah region and higher officials and dignitaries of the Muslim world twice a year. It is not intended for every day use. Some times it is opened for Muslim Leaders and Government guests.

In 1370 Hijri (AH) (1950 AD) the door with its frame was changed at the time of King Abdul Aziz Al Saud. It was made of wood and was Gold and silver plated with verses from the Holy Qur'an on it.

The second time it was replaced in the al Saud era was in (1983 AD) during the time of King Khaled Ibn Abdul Aziz Al Saud who after seeing that the gold plate on the door had dents and was torn in few places, ordered it to be replaced with a new door. The new door with its frame was completely made of pure gold, with Qur'anic verses inscribed and printed on it. At the bottom frame of the door inscribed the name of King Khaled Aal Saud, as the servant of the two holy mosques.

It has a lock and key especially designed and made in its original ancient style. The Key is about 1foot long and is kept in a specially made pouch, which is made of pure silk and gold embroidery along with the Kiswah. And it is always kept with the Aal Shaiby family who are the keepers of the house even before Islamic era. And prophet *Mohammad* (peace be upon him) has said that the Key shall always be kept with Aal Shaiby and that no one should take it from them. So it is kept with them through all generations in history.

The door of the Ka'abah. It is made of gold. It is made by King Khalid whose name inscribed on the door "Khalid ibin Abdul Aziz Al Saud –Servent of the two holy mosques"

The Ka'abah door covered with gold embroidered drapes is part of the whole shoud called the kiswah

THE KISWAH: (THE COVERING OF KA'ABAH)

The Kiswah is the black shroud which covers The Kaabah on all its four sides. It is made and knitted on handloom, from pure silk dyed in black, and manufactured in specially established factory for this purpose in Makkah. It is adorned with frames of calligraphic Arabic writing with verses from Holy Qur'an and Embroidered with pure silver and gold embroidery by Saudi Arabian Artisans specially trained for this purpose. And this Kiswah is changed once a year. King Fahad as the servant and custodian, takes special and personal interests in all the aspects of maintaining and providing the highest standard of maintenance and services in the two holy Mosques, and The Kaabah. The occasion of changing the Kiswah is the 9th of Dhu-Al-Hijjah when pilgrims are gathered in Arafat for Hajj, and it is the day before the celebration of Eid-ul-Adha. And so, even the Kaabah on Eid day glitters with its new worn dress, The Kiswah.

In the old days The Kaabah used to receive the Kiswah from the Othman rulers from Istanbul and later on it came from the Egyptian Governments and other Muslim countries, until the Saudi Government took over this responsibility and the honour to change the Kiswah. So, especially for this purpose, it established the factory near Makkah to make this black coloured covering every year.

THE WASHING OF THE KA'ABAH:

Before changing the new shrouds or the covering the Governor of Makkah region along with Princes, Ministers, Dignitaries and Heads of the Muslims diplomatic Missions and highest officials take pride in getting the honour of washing the inside of the Ka'abah. It is washed with Zam Zam water mixed with scents of highest quality, sandalwood and rose and oudah fragrance.

The ritual of washing the Ka'abah is done twice a year which is in the month of Sha'aban, in preparation for the coming month of Ramadan. And the second time it is washed in the month of Dhul Al Qi'dah which precedes the holy month of Hajj or the great pilgrimage.

CHAPTER
4

PURPOSE AND MAIN RITUALS
TOWARDS THE KA'ABAH

THE TWO MAIN RITUALS WHICH MUSLIMS PERFORM AROUND, AND FACING TOWARDS THE KAABAH:

The place where the Ka'abah was built by Prophet Ibrahim, was chosen long before humans came into existence. Prophet Ibrahim built the House on the foundations which was designated long before. This is indicated in the Qur'an in his prayer when he came the first time and left his wife and child over there in Makkah and mentioned in the Qur'an:

"Lord, I have settled some of my offspring in a barren valley near your sacred House." { 14:37}

And also with their prayers while they were building the house: And remember Abraham and Isamail while raising the foundations of the House, praying, our Lord, accept this service from us, for thou art the All Hearing and All knowing". { 2:127}

And also in this verse of the Qur'an:
The first House (of worship) appointed for mankind was that at Bakkah (the old name of Makkah) - (which is) full of blessings and guidance for all. { 3:96}

The Kaabah was built so that the people from all around the world will be united around it in their prayers and to worship God. It is the only direction Muslims face towards, while offering their prayers in one uniform way and procedure.

There are two main rituals which involves the Kaabah directly. Those are the Tawaf (to circumambulate) around it and the Salat (offering Prayers) facing towards it :

AL TAWAF: (THE CIRCUMAMBULATION) AROUND THE KAABAH:

When they come to visit this mosque, 'the Haram' Muslims go around this monument, seven times counter clock-wise, beginning from the corner where the Black Stone is fixed, keeping the Ka'abah on their left. This ritual is called the TAWAF, and it is done all the time, all the year round. In the Haram this is the greetings Muslims offer to the Ka'aabah and the Haram Mosque when they enter there. The Tawaf or circumambulation around the Ka'abah is an essential part of the Hajj (great pilgrimage), and also for the small pilgrimage called Omra. Without this Tawaf these two rituals becomes null and void.

AL SALAT: (OFFERING OF THE PRAYERS) FACING TOWARDS THE KA'ABAH:

The other most important ritual is called Al Salat, which is being done not only in this holy Mosque AL HARAM, but it is done and performed by all the Muslims from all around the world who turn to offer their prayers, and worship Allah facing towards it. Al Salat is the second corner or principle of Islam and it is performed five times a day. And because the time changes around the world so does night and day changes from place to place. For example, when it is day in the east, it is night in the west or vice -versa, so practically people around the world are facing and praying towards this Glorious Ka'aba, 24 hours a day, keeping in mind all the changes and the differences of the times because of the earths Meridians or time zones. In other words every minute some place some where some believers are bowing towards the Ka'abah offering their prayers and worshipping ALLAH – from around the world.

THE QIBLAH:

It is important to clarify to the readers, that Muslims Do Not worship the Ka'abah. For them it is the symbol of their unity, and the central point towards which they face from all over the world in their prayers. And that they worship Allah alone, in uniformity facing towards this house. The **Ka'abah** is the Qiblah for all Muslims. The Ka'abah is the center point of unity of Muslims, they face towards it five times a day obligatory prayers, and the direction from all around the world facing towards this Kaabah - is called the Qiblah.

When the Prophet of Islam came to Madinah he built the first mosque in Islam in the Quba'a area in the outskirts of Madinah. And then he built the second Mosque beside his house in the center of the city. There after many mosques were built in Madinah. In the beginning the Qiblah direction was towards the Al Aqsa Mosque in Jerusalem. But in the second year came the revelation to change the direction of the Qiblah towards the Ka'abah, in Makkah.

The revelations to change the Qibla thus mentioned in the Qur'an:

{2:144} **Many a time have We seen you"1"turn your face towards heaven. We will make you turn towards a qiblah that will please you. Turn your face towards the Holy Mosque; wherever you"2"be, (to all Muslims) turn your faces towards it. (The Ka'abah)** ("1"*Mohammad* **"2" The Faithful).**

And from that time the Qiblah is established towards the Ka'abah in Makkah and Muslims continue facing towards it while offering their Prayers.

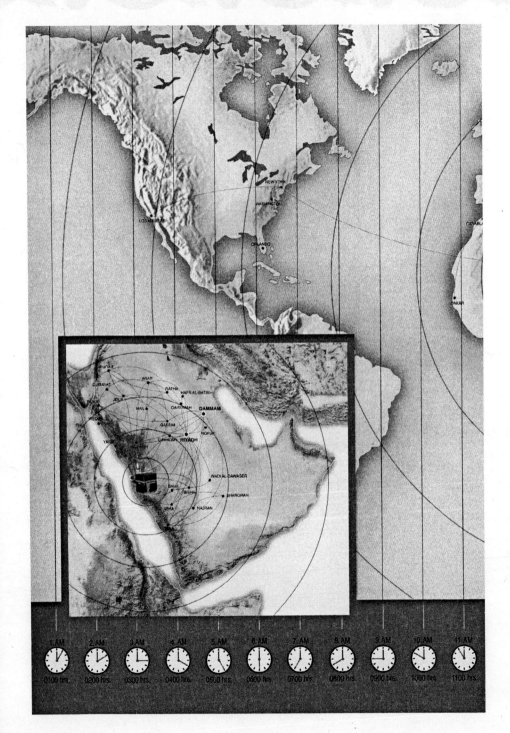

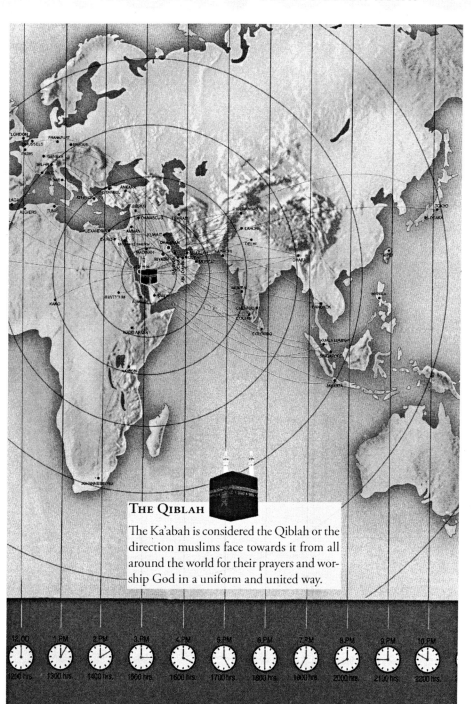

THE QIBLAH

The Ka'abah is considered the Qiblah or the direction muslims face towards it from all around the world for their prayers and worship God in a uniform and united way.

CHAPTER 5

THE ZAM ZAM SPRING WATER

THE DISAPPEARANCE OF ZAM ZAM SPRING:

After a very long time since it was first dug and sprang by the Angel for prophet Ibrahim's son and wife, the spring well of Zam Zam was buried by a leader of Jorham tribe during its war with another powerful tribe (when he was retreating after his defeat), He also buried his treasure consisting of statues, and other objects made of gold along with gold bullions, coins or nuggets in it. Probably he lost the war and was killed in the battle. And so the spring well and the treasure in it was forgotten, and with passing of time its where-about or location was lost and forgotten.

THE WATER SUPPLY IN MAKKAH:

The water scarcity in Makkah, especially during the pilgrimage seasons, when thousands of people comes there, made it a hardship for the people of Makkah. It was more so to the Bani Hashim tribes who are the descendants of Ismaeel, son of the Prophet Ibrahim (pbuh) and who were the rulers or chief tribes of Makkah at that time, the most respected sect in the Quraish tribe. It was their responsibility to see to the welfare and well being of the pilgrims coming to Makkah. Foremost of their concern and duties was to provide water which was scarce, and which they had to secure from wells dug out side Makkah.

THE DREAM:

Abdul Muttalib, the Grand father of Prophet *Mohammad* (pbuh) one day saw a dream in which he was ordered to dig "Taiba". He asked what is Taiba? But the dream ended without answer. He woke up not knowing what to do or where to dig. Again, the second and third nights he had similar dreams where the caller came again in his dreams and ordered him to dig, giving different names every night. He would ask what and where to dig, without getting a reply. The fourth night the caller came in the dream and asked him to dig Zam Zam. He asked what and where Zama Zam is. He was told, it is the spring well that will not diminish and its water will not finish, as it will flow for-ever, it will be for the drinking of the great pilgrimage. It is a dream from heaven, in this dream he was told the where-about of this spring well and did describe the place and where to dig for the Zam Zam water spring. It is in the same place where it first came to be when the Arch Angel Gabriel dug it with the flaps of his wings or the thump of his foot for the child Isamael, son of Prophet Ibrahim. It is besides the house of God, The Kaabah.

THE DREAM CAME TRUE:

Abdul Muttalib, rediscovered and dug out this spring-well after he saw in his dream the place and where-about of this spring. He and his only son at the time, Al Hareth, took the axe and shovel to dig the place. In the beginning they were resisted by other tribe members to dig and excavate near the Kaaba, but because he was the head and tribal chief of the Banu Hashim clan, the resistance stopped, with the agreement that they all will get a share of what-ever comes out of their digging. He and his son started digging. Very soon they found out the treasure of gold which was burried in there when this spring-well was buried and filled long times ago by the leader of Jorham tribe. And after digging further they struck the ZamZam spring again.

It was a clear and fresh spring water, and it is flowing since then, which is about 1500 years ago. This is one of the great Miracles. The Zama Zam water is believed to be the holiest water on earth. And it has a special qualities no other water has, it has the characteristic of a full nutritional diet, as people have survived for a long time without eating food except drinking this water. It is also known and recommended for its curing abilities of many ailments according to what a person would believe in. Because belief is the most important factor which might transform the dreams into reality by the will of God.

THE ORIGIN OF ZAM ZAM WATER:

Besides the many places it is flowing from inside the well and from many sides and directions of the well, the main place the Zam Zam water gushes out and originates from among the rocks which are under the east corner of the Kaabah, and below the corner stone.

An experiment done in 1400 Hijri AH (1980 AD) made by a group of scholars and scientists headed by a Saudi Engineer) shows how fast and how much the spring well is being fed from its tributaries which are among the different sides of the spring.

Four powerful water pumps were allowed to work on this spring-well with the velocity of 8000 liters per minute to empty the well. The water level at the mouth of the spring well is about 3.25 meters deep. A reading was taken every 30 seconds and when the water level reached the low height of 13.39, the pumping was stopped. Within 11 minutes the well was refilled up to 3.90 meters from its mouth. The engineer says "I will never forget the sight of the great scene when the water started gushing from all sides of the well with the tremendous force and volume, and the sound was unbearable." The well itself is about 30 meters deep. And the water level stays about 3.5 to 4.0 meters from the mouth of the well.

Originally the well had an entrance and a well-house near the Kaabah in the East. And since it was becoming difficult to pass by it due to congestion during the Tawaf and because of the increase in number of pilgrims, the entrance was closed and leveled with Tawaf area and it is covered with marble, people could walk and do the

Tawaf over it. The exact location, and its place is readily recognized by the sign imprinted on its site, about 18 meters from the Ka'abah facing the corner stone. The entrance to the well area was removed further to the east from the tawaf area and a new and well developed underground entrance was made where people can get in the well area and drink cool Zam Zam water from taps after being refrigerated and cooled and wash themselves with it.

In recent time the numbers of pilgrims and worshippers increased many folds. Besides the Hajj (or pilgrimage) period, there are millions who come for Omra during the whole year and especially during the month of Ramadan, when it becomes peak time for Omra. To make it convenient for them to do the Tawaf and perform the prayers without hindrance and obstruction it was planned by the Government to close the present entrance also and make it level with Tawaf area, so the Haram Tawaf area would become wider for the ever increasing number of visitors to the Haram.

As this book is coming to its end, this new plan has already been done and completed. The whole Tawaf area has been cleared, and became more roomy and spacious. There is no more Zam Zam spring-well underground entrance. Pilgrims may now drink cold Zam Zam water from taps connected to the walls at the far end of the tawaf area.

CHAPTER 6

ISLAM AND IT'S TEACHINGS

WHO ARE THE MUSLIMS?

After reading about Zam Zam spring, the Ka'abah and how and why it was built, and the importance and reverence Muslims gives to the Ka'abah comes the main and most important question; who are the Muslims? and what do they believe in.

Muslims constitutes a large sect of people throughout the world. They are part of each and every society and country. They believe in the oneness of God and *Mohammad* as His messenger and Islam as their religion. They observe the teachings of Islam and adhere to its principles and rituals, wherever they are.

The religion of Islam began in Makkah when the first revelations came to Prophet *Mohammad* about the year (611AD) in Makkah. In the beginning it was not received and accepted readily. At first it was ignored, but then it was fiercely resisted. And it really started to spread on quickly from Madinah and throughout the Arabian Peninsula at the time of the Prophet of Islam *Mohammad* (peace be upon him) after he migrated and settled in there in the year (622AD)

During the time of his successors the Caliph Rashdeen (The Pouise Succesors) – it spread well beyond Arabia and into north and West Africa and Asia Minor until it reached Bokhara Samarqand and Tashkent.

Countries could be occupied by force, but the religion, beliefs or ideologies cannot be forced or imposed on the people or nations there-in, for indefinite period, without their consent.

But because of its sanctity and the purity, and the justice, and equality and the kindness they found in it people joined in vast numbers to this religion every where. And as such we see that Islam spread throughout the world from China and Indonesia in the far-east until the Americas in the far-west, and from Russia in the north until South Africa and Australia in the south and all the places in between. They observe the teachings of Islam and adhere to its principles and rituals, wherever they are.

WHAT IS ISLAM?

Islam is the religion which believes in, and propagates the Oneness of God, Allah, and its Prophet and messenger of God, *Mohammad* (peace be upon him) who preached and propagated this belief, and taught its followers the way to worship God.

It is the final commandments and the completion of all divine religions which came before it. It confirms their teachings, like the ten commandments, and complements and completes their messages. It is the continuation of the religion of Islam propagated by Prophet Ibrahim (peace be upon him) the dean and father of most of the prophets and messengers of Allah. And the most important teachings of Islam is the **firm belief in the Oneness of God, and that** Mohammad **is the Messenger of Allah. This is the main message of the religion of Islam.** And then comes the rest of the teachings.

Islam is to propagate peace and harmony among people and nations without discrimination of race, color, creed and social levels or standards:

> **"All of you are from ADAM, and ADAM is (created) from soil."**

And another important aspect of Islam is to advocate **justice and kindness** among the people.

As the divine religion it has two fundamental sides or aspects. One is the inner belief or faith and the other is the practical side where there are the obligations to be performed. These two fundamental aspects are but the two sides of the same coin - indivisible.

FAITH (AL-EMAN):

After accepting Islam as their religion and adhering to its five principles and performing the required rituals, Muslims should also believe in its divine teachings faithfully. The belief in the following seven articles are among the most important things that they must believe in.

These are :

I believe in Allah
and in His Angels
and in His Books (Bible, Tawrah, Qur'an)
and In all His Messengers,
and in the Judgment day
and in destiny (or fate,) good and bad from God Almighty.
and in the Resurrection, after death.

These are the things a Muslim must believe in. Muslims must believe in and respect all the prophets and messengers preceding Prophet *Mohammad* (peace be upon him)

WHAT ARE THE TEACHINGS OF ISLAM?

This is the practical part of the belief in Islam. Like any other religion, ideology and belief, Islam also has its own principles, rules, regulations and rituals which its followers should believe in, comply with, and adhere to: Thus to start with Islam have five fundamental rules which are considered the main corners or (pillars) of Islam. A Muslim who accepts and embrace Islam Must:

1.   Believe that there is no god but Allah, and *Mohammad* is His servant and Messenger.

2.   Offer Prayers - (Five times a day)

3.   Pay the Zakat (Tax), due for the poor.

4.   Observe Fasting during the month of Ramadan.

5.   Perform the pilgrimage (Hajj), if and when able.

These principle beliefs and rituals are explained as follows:

1. BELIEVE AND ACCEPT THAT THERE IS NO GOD BUT ALLAH AND MOHAMMAD IS HIS MESSENGER:

After accepting and believing in this first and the most fundamental corner of Islam, which is the One-ness of God, and in *Mohammad* as God's Prophet, a person becomes Muslim.

Then as good followers of this religion, Muslims would believe in, accept and adhere to, and observe the other four corners (or pillars), which are rituals, and are to be offered and performed. These are the practical part of the belief, and are as follows:

2. AL SALAAT (OFFERING OF PRAYERS):

The ritual of doing the Salawat or prayers. It is the second corner or principles of Islam. And it is established on Muslims when Prophet *Mohammad* (peace be upon him) was raised to heaven - where he was bestowed-upon this ritual which is to be performed by the believers. These prayers are offered and performed at their designated time, and not before. It is mentioned in the Qur'an thus: **Verily, al Salat (prayer) is enjoined on the believers at fixed time.**(Al-Nissa-103).

These prayers are obligatory and are done five times a day as follows:

1.   **Salat Al-Fajr:** which means "morning" prayers, and its time starts or begins from the break of dawn until sunrise only. It is offered in two voluntary and two compulsory Rakaat's (bowing down towards Qibla – which is the direction to the Kaabah in Makkah).

2. **Salat Al-Dhohor:** It means "Noon"prayers. And its time is from noon until afternoon. It is four voluntary, four compulsory, and two voluntary Rakaats. (Noon time is when the sunshine is on top of a person or a pole and there is no shadow except beneath it. Once the shadow starts and the sun moves towards west the time of Dhor Prayer begins.)

3. **Salat Al-Asr:** It means "afternoon" Prayers. And its time is from afternoon until sunset. It is four compulsory Raka'ats only. (Afternoon or Asr time is approximately measured when the shadow becomes bigger than the person or the pole)

4. **Salat Al-Maghreb:** It means after "sunset" prayers, atnd its time is immediately after sunset until night. It is three compulsory; and two voluntary Raka'ats.

5. **Salat Al-Isha:** Which means the "night" prayers, and its time starts about one and half hour after the Maghreb prayer time, and it may extend until late at night. And it is four compulsory + two + three voluntary Raka'ats.

SALAT AL JOMA'A (FRIDAY PRAYER):

Friday is a special day for Muslims. It is a holiday where Muslims offer special prayer, and a festive day that people may enjoy and rest after a weeks work.

Every week there is a special prayer offered on Friday around noon time, which substitute the Dhohor (Zohor) prayer on that day. It is an obligatory (or Fardh) prayer to be offered by Muslim men on that day, in congregation. It consist of two Raka'ats before which the Emam makes a sermon or Khutba.

Muslims should be clean, cut their nails and trim their hair and have the grand ablution (Ghosol), and wear neat dress before going to the Mosque to offer this prayer. Friday prayer must be offered in congreation in the mosque.

A person who misses this congregation due to valid reasons like sickness or traveling, or the women who prays in their home, will offer the Dhohor prayer instead, like the rest of the week days.

PRAYER TIMINGS:

The salawt or offering of prayers is the most important ritual that should be done by all Muslims, young and old, men and women, even sick persons are not relieved of this obligation and must perform it, even if they have to do it while lying in their sick-bed.

Prayer timing are well defined and designated. It is essential that the prayers are offered and done only after its time commenced or entered and not before, otherwise it is considered void, and then it should be offered and performed within its proper time limits. But in certain circumstances like when a person forgets and or overslept unintentionally he/she may offer the past prayers the time they may remember it or when they wake up from their sleep. Also during travel these times can be slightly varied and can be offered in combinations, and also shortened. This will be explained later, in the convenience or concession chapter (#8) in the book.

Although it is allowed to be performed anywhere, men are obliged and encouraged to offer their prayers in congregation, and in the mosques.

Only women are relieved of this and other religious obligations, when they are in their menstruation period and for the full duration and days of their period.Women are also exempted from, and are not obliged to offer the congregational prayers. They may offer all their prayers in their home. But, if they wish they may go to the mosque to join congregation, in the women's section. The Prophet had said "Do not prohibit (or forbid) the women who worship God from going to the houses of God".

Offering of (Salat) is the ritual that defines Muslims and differentiates them from non Muslims.

3. PAYING THE ZAKAT (TAX DUES FOR THE POOR):

Giving the Zakat. It is a duty on all Muslim people who may have money and richness exceeding the poverty limit (which is about the equivalent of 85 grams of Gold), and they are obliged to pay about 2½ % of their accumulated and stored richness, which was kept for one whole year without being used or put to work. The Zakat is paid to the Government who would use it for the benefit of the people and distribute it among its poor and needy ones, and or could be paid directly to the people who are categorized and mentioned in the Qur'an:

Sadaqat (Alms- charitable donations)) are for [1] **the poor and** [2] **the destitute; for those that** [3] **are engaged in the management of alms and** [4] **those whose hearts are sympathetic to the Faith; for** [5] **the freeing of slaves and** [6] **debtors; for** [7] **the advancement of God's cause; and for** [8] **the traveler in need. That is a duty enjoined by God. God is all-knowing and wise.** { 9:60}

The note: (1-8 are the categories of the poor and needy people to whom the Zakat is payable),

Zakat or Alms Tax is distributed and given to the eight categories of poor and needy people as mentioned in the above verse in the Qur'an. Among them mentioned are the poor, destitutes and also the ones who are managing and working for the disbursement and distributing of this tax. Also this Zakat could be used to pay the debt of the ones who are unable to repay the loans they obtained, and the traveler who has nothing left to pay for his living and way back fare. Zakat, if paid properly could alleviate many social problems and pains felt by the poor, in the society. It is sharing of the rich people with the poor alleviating some of their pain and misery.

This verse explains that zakat may be paid only these people: the poor and the needy in order to improve their situation and let them have a comfortable standard of living; the zakat administrators so that the zakat institution should be self financing; and those whose support we want to win for the Islamic cause.

This group could be newcomers to Islam, or non-Muslims who are sympathetic to Islam.

The other four groups are paid for a purpose, which means that we can ensure that the purpose is served, rather than the payment is paid to them directly. In the case of an insolvent debtor, you could give your zakat to his creditors in repayment of his debts. Similarly, for a traveler in need, we could buy a train or plane ticket to take him home.

Islam tries to overcome the social problems by facing them directly and not by ignoring or avoiding them. By accepting or recognizing the presence or the existence of the problems, it becomes easy to solve it. The social and economical imbalance in societies is not new. But the way Islam solves it is unique. There are few practical solutions presented to solve or alleviate this strong Socioeconomic problem:

1.   Zakat is among the most important solution and it is an obligatory (compulsory) part or corner of Islam. It is imposed on the rich to alleviate the immediate needs and requirements of the poor and needy, and helps them financially.

2.   The other method of helping and providing for the poor is to encourage and assist people in making personal contributions, and these are the sadaqat or the charities. And it is a voluntary subscription of the rich people to help in the society's poor and their needs and it is strongly encouraged and welcomed.

Islam encourages all works and payments of charities and makes incentive for all what is paid in the name of Allah and promises a good rewards in this world and a higher place in the world after, which we all are required to seek.

For each good deed we do in our lifetime for our fellow people Allah promises to give rewards ten times and up to seven hundred times more and up to unlimited awards. **And Islam asks people to be kind and helpful to each other in every society.**

Charities and Zakat cannot be paid to anyone whom we are required to support, such as our own wives, children or parents, because we are obliged to take care of them and their welfare.

[With all the solutions given to this problem Islam does not encourage the idleness or laziness or avoiding of work. Instead it emphasizes on the hard working labour and doing the perfect job when given the work and the opportunity to do a job. And this is why it also strongly emphasize on giving the labour his full salary/wages even before his sweat dries out to show the seriousness for giving his remuneration on time and in full for his labour and services.]

4. SOUM RAMADAN (FASTING DURING THE MONTH RAMADAN):

It is the fourth part or corner or pillar of Islam. It is a compulsory ritual, and it is done during the day for one complete month, the month of Ramadan, which is the holy month for Muslims. Ramadan is the month where-in the revelation of the holy Qur'an began. Muslims would keep fasting and do not eat, drink, do or desire sex, or smoke from dawn until sunset during this month. They abstain from doing all these cravings for all day long. After sunset normal life starts where they can eat and drink and do the usual daily routine until next dawn, when fasting starts again for all day long.At night after Isha prayers, a voluntary prayer called the Taraweeh is offered by muslims every where.

And in a Hadith Qudsi Allah informs his messenger Prophet *Mohammad* (peace be upon him) that "All the work humans pursue for themselves except the Fasting, as it is (done) for me and I am giving the reward for it."

Fasting is performed during this month by all able bodied people and youngsters who became adults. There are exceptions or concessions for sick persons who because of their ill health or weakness are unable to do the fasting, travelers who are away from their home place, and women in their menstrual period. But they all have to compensate and fast for all the days they could not fast in this month. They should do this compensation, at their convenience, during the rest of the year and whenever they are able to do it. Very old and terminally sick or ill persons who cannot do the fasting are required to feed a poor person an average meal for all the days they could not fast.

5. Performance of Hajj (It is the fifth part or corner of Islam)

Doing the Hajj or pilgrimage to Makkah It is also a compulsory and obligatory ritual Muslims must do it once in their lifetime, whenever they are able to do so mentally, physically and economically. The way to do this ritual is explained in the next chapter.

CHAPTER
7

HAJJ

WHAT IS HAJJ?

Hajj is the 5th fifth corner or principle of Islam. It is a ritual which should be performed once in a lifetime, if and when a person is able to do so. It is scheduled once in a year at a designated period of time. Because it is a ritual which involves hardship and discomfort, it is made obligatory only once in a life time for the Muslims to do, and only for those who can perform or are able to do it - it applies: The ability is defined in the Qur'an thus:

"Pilgrimage to the House is a duty to God on mankind who can make it. (those who can afford its means to do it). [3:97]

When Prophet Abraham finished building the Ka'abah he was told to call for people to visit this house:

"And announce among mankind to do the hajj, they will come to you on the back of swift/lean animals from every distant quarter, they will come to avail themselves of many a benefit and to pronounce on the appointed days the name of God over the cattle which He has given them for food. Eat of their flesh, feed the poor and the unfortunate."[22:27]

And he did announce this message loudly in the valley of Makkah. And the call of Prophet Abraham (peace be upon him) by the grace and will of God reached every where and every distant quarter and place, and since then people or mankind started visiting this house for pilgrimage.

This pilgrimage in Islam is known as the Hajj. This ritual was performed by Prophet *Mohammad* (peace be upon him), once in his lifetime before his death on the 11th year(AH), after his migration to Madinah.

The Hajj consists of five important or essential parts which are:

1.   The wearing of Ehram at or abeam the designated places, and before entering the borders of Makkah, which are called the Meeqats of Hajj or Omra.

2.   The visit to the Kaabah and doing the Tawaf orcircumambulate around it, seven rounds.

3.   Sa'aei or the striving between Al Safa and Al Marwa hills seven times.

4.   The most important and THE ESSENTIAL part of Hajj is to be in ARAFAT on the 9th day of the hajj month.

5.   The shaving or shorting of the hair.

There are other rituals to be done in Mina, which are also part of the Hajj, like the throwing of stones on the Shaitan (Satan) effigy or symbol and the sacrifice of cattle, which will be explained later-on in this chapter. There are the months of Hajj when people would come and stay in Makkah after Ramadan to perform Hajj. These months are Shawal and zul-Q'eda.

The Hajj is performed and limited to a period of time in the year (six days in the month of Dhu Al Hijjah) from the 8th till the 13th of the month of Dhu Al Hijjah.

THE EHRAM:

One of the most important and essential part to perform Hajj (pilgrimage) or Omrah the (small pilgrimage) is the wearing of an apparel consisting of two sheets of cloth called the Ehram. One sheet is worn around the waist, like a (skirt or kilt) in the west, or the (sarong or lungi) in the east. And the other sheet is worn or put over the shoulder to cover the upper body. These are the only apparel men will wear besides the open sided footwear.

It symbolizes the uniform out look of men who come to Makkah to perform these rituals and rites, and thus there becomes no distinction between the wealthy or the poor. The women wears their normal but wide, loose and not transparent dress, which would not define their body or show any part of it, except for their face and their hands which may be left uncovered.

The Ehram should be worn at or before the nominated places designated by Prophet *Mohammad* (peace be upon him) before entering the Haram area or boundary of Makkah. And these places are called the Meeqat.

THE MEEQATS:

There are five places which were designated by Prophet *Mohammad* (peace be upon him), where pilgrims should change their dress and wear their Ehram at or abeam these places before entering the areas of Makkah to perform Hajj or Omra. And these place are called the Meeqat places and are designated as follows:

1. **Meeqat Dhul Hulaifah:** This place is designated for the people living in Madinah and its surrounding area, and for the ones coming via Madinah from the north like from Turkey, Syria etc. This place is commonly known as Abyar Ali now, and it is in the outskirt of Madinah on the way to Makkah. It is about 450 km from Makkah.

2. **Meeqat Al Johfah:** It is for the people coming or passing through from the North -West i.e.- from Europe, North Africa, North America etc. It is near or abeam the port of Rabigh - about 185 km from Makkah.

3. **Meeqat Qarrn Al Manazil:** This is the place for the people coming from the East, It is North of Taif about 75 Km from Makkah.

4. **Meeqat Yalamlam:** This is where people coming from Yemen or from the South would use, it is about 92 km from Makkah

5. **Meeqat Dhat (Zat) Irq:** For the People coming from Iraq or there about, or the North East. It is about 90 Km North East of Makkah area.

Those are the designated places for people coming on land transport and who will be passing by and stop there to have their Ghosul or ritual ablution to remove impurity, and change their cloths into the Ehram apparel.

And then offer and call or announce their submission to worship Allah in the ritual of Hajj or Omrah. This call of Submission is essential and it is called the Niyah (or intention) and Talbiya (announcing their acceptance or compliance). These places are well maintained to facilitate the pilgrims to do their Ghosul or cleaning ritual and change into the Ehram.

Muslims may choose to put on their Ehram apparel before leaving their homes, but it is essential to make the Talbiyah or announcement of their intentions for Hajj and/or Omra before passing these places or passing abeam it.

PASSING OVER OR ABEAM THE MEEQATS BY AIR:

Unlike the land transport there are hundreds of flights daily coming from all around the world into the Jeddah Airport, (which is the main gate-way to Makkah), before they proceed to Makkah. The Airplanes does not necessarily pass-over these Meeqats. It may be flying in different paths or airways. And the air ways or paths of the flights does not necessarily pass-over those Meaqats exactly, but may pass abeam it. And according to Saudi Government the flight crew should announce or show in their video channels the estimated time to arrive at and pass over or abeam any of those five Meaqat points. When the pilgrims or passengers know about this time they will recite or announce the niyah and talbiya on or before the designated or expected time to pass the Meeqat.

Because of the variation in the distance and time of the flight to pass-over or abeam the meeqats, and also because of the flying conditions like turbulence and the weather enroot, the flight could deviate from its original course and assume another flight path. These and other unexpected and uncomfortable flying conditions and other circumstances like the congestion and insufficient or inadequate Ghosul or purifying areas in the airplane, may make it difficult for the pilgrims to change their dress into the Ehram garments inside the airplane during the flight, and may make them forget the Niyah or Talbiya, or the crew forgets to announce the passage time over or abeam these Meeqats. Therefore it is advisable that pilgrims do wear their Ehram cloths before boarding the airplanes or before leaving their homes, and may make the announcement of Niyah and Talbiya when the flight begins so that there would be no more confusion occurs on the way, and they would not miss doing these necessary parts of their Hajj or Omra rituals.

Also, sometimes the meeqat time or place comes in the immediate vicinity of the departure airport like Madinah airport, where there may be no time to do anything before the flight passes away from meeqat. And on another flights it may take hours before the flight carrying the Hajis or pilgrims passes by the meeqat, like when it is coming from the far east or the far west. So it is good idea to avoid all that confusion and observe and do what is supposed to be done well in time. Because if a Haji or pilgrim passes the Meeqat, and enters the boundary of the Haram without being fully prepared, and changed his clothes into Ehram apparel, and did not do the Niyah and Talbiya, he have to offer a sacrifice of sheep in Makkah area to adjust or compensate for the omission or fault and mistake, and make up for his hajj or Omra to be complete.(see meeqat map: p).

So it will be a good idea that pilgrims attain or put on their Ehram garments befor they leave their homes after having made their Ghosul, and announce their intension (niyah) for Haj or Omra while boarding the airplane or at the beginning of the flights. This will save them lots of confusions or omissions during the flight.

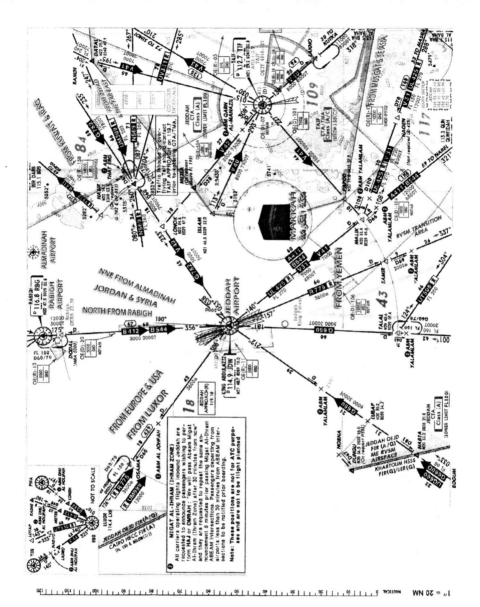

NOTE: There is no airport in Makkah. All arriving flights land in Jeddah Airport, which is the gateway to Makkah.

2. Ehram zones are points designated on the flying charts.

WHAT IS NIYAH & TALBIYAH?

Niyah is the intention to do or carryout some function i.e. I intend to perform Hajj and or Omra. The intention may be made silently in our mind or announced so that we know and confirm to ourselves what we are planning to do initially, while preparing ourselves for the duties we are intending to do: perform Hajj or Omra or both. Niyah is very important in carrying out and performing any obligation or duties to perform. For instance we intend to perform Hajj and or Omra, I intend to perform the salawt (prayers), I intend to pay the zakat, I intend to keep fast tomrrow etc. etc. And as mentioned earlier intentions are necessary to perform any obligation or duty regardless if it is made silent inside our mind or announced openly or verbally.

"Actions (or deeds) are preceded by intentions. And everyone will get the rewards of what he intended to do." These are from Hadith of the Prophet (peace be upon him).

Talbiya is the formal announcement of submission or acceptance in response to the heavenly call of Hajj or Omra. And it is done after the Ghosul or purification and putting on the ehram apparel. After the intention (Niyah) have been made for Hajj or Omra then the Talbiya is done and announced openly as follows:

Labbaik Allahoumma Labbaik
Labbaika La shareeka Laka Labbaik
Enna Al Hamda, wa Al Ne'mata, Laka wa Al Mulk –
La Shareeka Lak.

Which literally means:

(At Your services our Lord (Allah) – At Your service O Lord Who have no partner - All the praise, all the bounties are but for You and the kingdom belongs to You - There is no one to share with You).

STARTING OF THE RITUAL OF HAJJ

After arriving in Makkah the Pilgrims (Hajis):

1.   Should do the Tawaf and the Sa'ee i.e.: The circumambulation around the Kaabah seven rounds, and the hurrying or striving in between the AlSafa and Marwa hill (which are now inside the Haram) also seven times, back and forth.

2.   Proceed on the 8th day of the month to Mina where they would stay overnight. And from here the six day hajj already begun.

ARAFAT

And From Mina they proceed the next day (the 9th of Dhu Al Hijjah) to Arafat. To be in this place (ARAFAT) is a must and compulsory for **performing the Hajj.** If the Haji or pilgrim does not visit and stay in Arafat on this date (the 9th of Hajj) until after sunset his Hajj is not complete and it will be null and void, because as the prophet says "The Hajj is Arafat". On this date, all the pilgrims shall gather in ARAFAT. And by being in Arafat on this date (9th of Hajj) pilgrims will have attained and completed the most important part of this ritual. Arafat is in a big valley about 22km east of Makkah. The Hajis stay in Arafat from morning until after sunset, where they spend the day worshipping Allah and praying. Here is Jabal Al Rahma or "Mountain of Mercy"

On his pilgrimage the Prophet came to Arafat. He then offered the Dhohar and Asr Prayers combined (and performed it two Raka'at each) in congregation in the place where today Masjid Namerah (mosque) is situated. And while in Arafat, Prophet *Mohammad* (peace be upon him) went and climbed on Mount Rahmah and gave his fare well speech, where in he said that it may be the last time for him to be there and with them again. This was an indication that he may not live longer and his friends and companions understood this reference, and became sad and felt it. And he emphasized on Muslims to live in a brotherly manner and not to kill each other or anyone else, unlawfully. He emphasized on the Muslims to take care and treat the Ansars of Madinah well, because they were the hosts and supporters of the Muslim Mahajreen (immigrants) who came from Makkah empty handed, and the ansar's treated them with great hospitality and generosity. He also emphasized on the good treatment of women, and described the women as (fragile) like flask; tender human beings, they are sisters of the men and should be treated as such with respect and care. He said he is leaving with them two things that if they stand with and adhere to, they will not go astray and would not lose the right path ever. Those two things he described were the Qur'an the divine book, and to follow his footsteps and his teachings.

HAJJ 6 DAYS

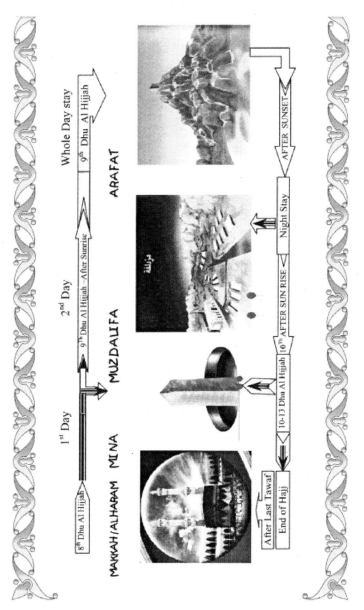

The throwing of stones (pebbles)

The Jamarat or the satanic walls which were built recently. It symbolizes the effigy of Satan and the pilgrims throw pebbles on it, following the example of Prophet Ibrahim (peace be upon him).

MUZDALIFAH

After Sunset pilgrims proceed from Arafat towards Muzdalifah on their way back to Mina. This is a valley before Mina, where they offer the two prayers of Maghreb and Isha (shortened two rakáat) combined, and then camp overnight until the beginning of dawn next day - After offering their dawn prayer, (on the 10th of Dhu Al Hijjah) they would proceed to mina again. In Muzdalifah the pilgrims pickup pebbles stones to take it with them to Mina where they will offer the symbolic ritual of throwing the stones, like Prophet Abraham did, when he threw pebbles onto satan.

MINA

And from Muzdalifah pilgrims proceed to Mina. The first thing to do in Muna is to go to the place called the grand Jamarat where they throw seven pebbles on the symbolic monument of satan following the footsteps of Prophet Abraham when he threw stones on the satan. Satan followed prophet Abraham in Mina to incite him against the will of God and to discourage him from sacrificing his son Ismail - which Prophet Abraham was commanded to do in his dreams.

Mina is a place about 8-10 km east of Makkah. It is the first stage when proceeding to perform Hajj on the 8th of Dhu- Al- Hajj,and also the last stage, before completing the Hajj. which is the 10th, 11th and 12th Dhul-Hajj.

After visiting and staying in Arafat on the 9th, the Hajis or pilgrims start their return trip back after sunset and spend the next night camping in the open air in Muzdalifah, and in the morning of (the 10th of Dhu-Al-Hijjah) they arrive in Muna again, where they will stay for the next three days camping under the newly built camps made of fire resistant fiber glass homes. These are adequately equipped camps built in place of the old system of tents which could, and did

catch fire many times in the past. There is the coolant air condition-
ers and running water available in all camps at Mina. This made the
Hajj or pilgrimage more convenient than it was in the old days, when
people would be camping in inconvenient tents and more hazardous
situations created with the ever increasing number of the pilgrims
coming here yearly. There is a modern slaughter house where pilgrims
may delegate their sacrifice to be done on their behalf. There are the
three symbolic monuments of satan which pilgrims throw pebbles
on during their stay following the footstep and example of Prophet
Abraham and Prophet *Mohammad* (peace be upon them and upon
all the Prophets and messengers of Allah).

In the last two or three days of staying or camping in Mina pilgrims would perform three rituals in whichever order it is convenient
for them, which are:

1.   The stoning or throwing of the pebbles on the three satanic
poles which are built by bricks and stones and symbolizes the effigy
of satan. This custom is in tradition with the act of prophet Ibrahim
who threw stones at the satan when he saw him at these three places
to incite him from doing his rituals, and disobey the commands he
was given by God.

2.   Shaving of the head or shortening of the hair. The most desir-
able is to shave the head for men, which prophet *Mohammad* (peace
be upon him) himself did, and preferred.

3.   To do the sacrifice and slaughter if required i.e.; for some pilgrims it is required to do the sacrifice like the ones who would perform
Hajj in Tamatou or Qiran methods.

After performing any or all of these rituals the pilgrims may release
themselves of the Ehram, and this way it is deemed that he/she have completed most part of their Hajj rituals. They may now wear their normal
dress. The only restriction they have is their marriage relation, which is not
allowed until they complete fully their Hajj by visiting Makkah and do

the Tawaf Al Efadah. That will completes their Hajj performance. From now on they would be starting a new pious and righteous life among their people and society and the world at large.

After completing the Hajj rites peacefully a person would consider himself a new born Muslim. Because according to a saying (hadith) of Prophet *Mohammad* (peace be upon him) which means "That whoever performed Hajj without being offensive and did not argue (unnecessarily) or did a bad deed, he returns back like the time his mother gave birth to him". New born - nice and clean slate! Forgiven all the previous wrong doings. Now he starts a new life where in he should try not to do any bad deed, and improvise his actions and attitude to become a good person. It is not so hard or difficult. All what we have to do is; give it a try!

In spite of all the difficulties, hardship and inconvenience a Muslim may have encountered during the performance and offerings of the Hajj rites and rituals, it is important that he should keep himself under control and abstain from doing obscenity, wicked-ness, wrangling (arguing) so as not to lose the rewards for all this hardship he went through and it may become void or in-vain. Thus it is mentioned in the Quràn:

The Hajj is (in) **the well-known months.** (the 10th month, the 11th month and the first ten days of the 12th month of the Islamic calendar, i. e. two months and ten days). **So whosoever intends to perform Hajj, then he should not have sexual relations** (wife/husband). **nor commit sin, nor dispute unjustly during the Hajj. And whatever good you do, Allah knows it. And take a provision for the journey, but the best provision is At-Taqwa** (piety, righteousness). **So fear Me, O men of understanding!** (2:197)

THE SACRIFICE: AL ADHA

In one of his visits to Makkah, Prophet Ibrahim saw in his dreams that he was commanded by Allah to sacrifice his son Ismaeel. This was a great test between the fatherly love and the obedience of the command of God. He told his son about this dream, and his son Ismaeel was as obedient to God's commands as his father was. He did not disobey or refuse. He told his father to obey and carry out the command he had received from God, without reluctance. And it is mentioned in the Quran:

(Abraham said) My Lord grant me (offspring) from the righteous* So we told him of the good news of a forbearing boy (gentle son)* And when he reached the age he could work with him his father said O my son, I see in my dream that I am slaughtering you, tell me what Is your view, (what do you think?), He said O my father, Do as you Are commanded. God willing you will find me steadfast*

And when they both had submitted to the will of God, and he laid down his son on his face,* WE called him - O Abrahim, you have (believed) fulfilled the dream, and thus WE reward the righteous.* That was indeed a great test.* And WE ransomed him with a great sacrifice.* And WE left for him a (good) remembrance among later generations.* Peace be upon Ibrahim.* (Al Saffat 100-109)

And when Prophet Ibrahim put the knife on his son's neck to slaughter him, God's Angels replaced or ransomed his son and put a sheep instead, under his knife, and Prophet Ibrahim slaughtered the sheep. Both Father and son passed this hard test of obedience very well. And so began the ritual of slaughtering the sheep or cattle during the performance of Hajj in Muna. At the same time this sacrifice is also done around the world during the festival period of Eid Al Adha, in celebration of this occasion. And according to their status people may sacrifice Lamb, Sheep, Cow or Camel, and distribute the meat among themselves as they give some to the poor, and some for themselves, their family, friends and neighbors.

OMRA (SMALL PILGRMAGE):

Omra is the small pilgrimage to Makkah It is limited to the circum-ambulation or Tawaf around the Ka"abah and the striving between the Alsafa and Al Marwa hills, Seven times.

Wearing the Ehram at or before the Meeqat is also an essential part of this ritual, and after completing the rites and offering their prayers the pilgrims should cut or shorten their hair. With this rite the Omra is complete and finished. Simple!

Omra may be performed throughout the year but the most well desired time to do it, is during the month of Ramadan, when its reward is being promised more abundantly. Omra is a voluntary deed and ritual.

THE VISIT TO MADINAH:

Muslims who come from all places and far corners of the world to perform Hajj and Omra in Makkah are likely, and will visit the Mosque of the Prophet in Madinah. This is a great wish and desire of Muslims to visit this Holy City which was the cradle of Islam, and from where Islam spread and where the Prophet of Islam Mohammad (Peace be upon him) died, and is buried. They may visit Madinah before or after performance of Hajj or Omra.

The Prophet have said which means: "There are three places which should be considered to visit. The holy Mosque (in Makkah), my Mosque (in Madinah) and the Aqsa Mosque (in Jerusalem)."

The Prophet of Islam Propet *Mohammad* (peace be upon him) was buried inside his own house. Later on when his friends and Caliph Abu Bakr and Omar died they also were burried beside him. And their tombs became part of, and inside the Mosque in Madinah.

Beside the prophets Mosques, there is the burial ground of "Jannat Al Baqie" in Madinah where there are many of the family members and relatives of the Prophet are buried. Besides them, there are also most of the Prophet's companions and friends most famous among them is Othamn Ibn Affan the third Caliph, the martyrs of Ohod, and the followers thereafter and many well known scholars of Islam are buried in Jannat Al Baqei.

Muslims visit Madinah and offer prayers in the Prophet's mosque and then, they offer tribute and salam to the Prophet of Islam *Mohammad* (peace be upon him) and his two companions, Abu Bakr and Omer who are buried beside him - inside this mosque. They also would visit the burial ground of Jannat Al Baqui. and pay tribute to the people buried over there and pray for them.

In Madinah there is The Quba'a Mosque which was the first Mosque built in Islam, and people are urged to visit and offer prayers in it, while they are in Madina, as the prophet (peace be upon him) used to go and pray in this mosque often.

TO PERFORM HAJJ/OMRA BY PROXY

Hajj and/or Omra are the only rituals which may be made by proxy i.e. on behalf of others. Someone who is at that time physically unable to perform it, or a dead person like the father or the mother to whom (or to their soul) we may offer the rewards of the Hajj we may perform. A bed ridden sick person who is physically unable to perform Hajj may delegate some one to do or perform Hajj on his/her behalf. He/She should provide the travel accommodation and living expenses to the person who is going to perform the Hajj on their behalf. The person who is being required to do the Hajj on their behalf should have had himself performed his own obligatory Hajj. Then he may perform the Hajj/Omra on behalf of anyone else. A person who himself have not done/ (performed) his own Hajj cannot perform Hajj on behalf of others.

Doing Hajj or Omra by others on some one's behalf may be done.

When someone due to any unforeseen reasons or physical ailment or inability could not do the Hajj personally. He/she may delegate someone to perform it on their behalf, during their life-time

A dutiful son or daughter may voluntarily want to do Hajj or Omra for their deceased father/mother may do so, especially for either of their parents who was unable to perform their obligatory Hajj during their lifetime. Because paying the dues for the obligatory rituals to God is important. We must also believe that whoever perform these rituals on behalf of others, will himself also benefit from the bounties reserved for these rituals as much as the one's they are doing this obligation for, by proxy or voluntarily.

The Hajj or Omra by proxy or on behalf of others could be done for one person at a time. It may not be done for more than one person at the same time. It should be done one at a time.

But if some one wants to perform Omra for his/her parents (father and mother). He may do Omra for one of them first, and afterwards or later, while he is in Makkah, he may proceed to the meeqat of the Makkah residents, which is the Taneem (or Omra Mosque), and there put on ehram and do the Niyah and Talbiyah for the other person or parent to do the Omra for. This way many Omra's could be performed.

CHAPTER 8

CONCESSION ON DOING THE PRAYERS AND OTHER RITUALS

CONCESSIONS ON DOING PRAYERS:

Islam is a practical and humanly religion. It does not impose undue burden or hardship on its followers When it made the religious rituals and obligations it also made some concessions on these rituals according to the circumstances.

There are some concessions granted on the compulsory obligations to worship God and offer the required prayers. A Muslim should perform these obligations as much as possible, and as his health condition would allow him. Islam is a religion which looks into the matters in a humanly manner and ways.

"GOD does not Impose (burden) on a soul beyond its scope" (2-285)

And at certain stages in life and due to the change in health, and due to sickness or travel, there are certain concessions on the compulsory obligations and duties, which are granted according to the situation required. These concessions are in the form of reducing the numbers of performance, but are valued as much as when it is performed in its full form and numbers.

The Prophet says - which means, that "God likes his concessions be taken (or adhered to), as much as he likes that His compulsory obligations are being adhered to." These authorized or permitted sanctions of reducing the obligatory prayers and also postponing some of the rituals are as follows:

PRAYING (AL SALAT) DURING TRAVEL:

The concession on this ritual is applied to the prayers of four raka'ats, which are reduced and may be performed two raka'ats. Besides the reduced number of Raka'ats it may also be combined, and offered two prayers at a time. And when using the combined form of prayers, then the prayer times are reduced to three times a day, instead of five times in the normal situations. This concession applies while traveling.

So Dohor prayer may be combined with Asr prayer and would be performed two raka'at each, and the Maghreb prayers could be combined with the Isha. There is no reduction for Maghreb prayers as it is already three raka'ats, but Isha prayer will be reduced to half and becomes two raka'ats.

Prayers have to be performed in all circumstances, even sick men must perform their prayers. If they cannot stand, they may pray while seated. If they cannot sit, they may pray while laying in their sick-bed and so forth.

The only exception given is for women. Women must not pray during their menstrual period at all, and are free and exempt from this obligation during their periods. They are also relieved from other religious obligations during this time. Also they are not required to compensate for the lost prayers which they did not perform during their menstrual period.

FASTING, ILLNESS AND OLD AGE:

When Muslims are traveling they are given the concessions/permission that they may not keep fasting during the days they are traveling and are away from home. They may avail this concession Allah have given to the travellers and they may not fast during their travel, regardless if the travel is streneous or otherwise.

Also if someone is sick, they are relieved from fasting during the month of Ramadan, if they cannot keep fasting due to the illness.

But when everything is Ok and they are back at home, and feel well, all the days which were not being fasted during the month of Ramadan should be compensated. The period for compensation is extended and are long enough, until the month of Ramadan, next year. Which means there are 11 months during which time they may do the compensation at their own convenience. But it should be done. The women who did not keep fasting due to their period in the month of Ramadan, are also required to compensate and do the fasting later.

Even though they have no specific illness, old age itself counts as an illness. When an elderly person finds fasting too strenuous to bear, he or she may not fast, but may compensate by feeding poor people. The two meals should be of the average type he and his family normally have.

Hajj:

The biggest concession is on Hajj (Pilgrimage to Makkah). Because the most important factor which makes Hajj compulsory are three, a person should be healthy, wealthy and wise. Part of this idiom does also apply on other religious duties.

If a person cannot afford the expenses of traveling to Makkah, besides leaving enough expense for his family and dependents, he is not obliged to perform Hajj. If his health is not well and he cannot perform hajj physically, then he is exempt from doing it, until he is good enough to be able to perform it. And if a person is insane, then all religious obligations are removed from this person until he becomes well and sane.

Zakat:

It is meant for people who are above the poverty level as explained earlier. And they should have a sufficient amount above this level with them for a whole year. Then they have to pay the Zakat, and only on the amount which is left with them for a complete one year.

So the concession applies to those who do not have the amount and the value at or above that level for the whole year, and they are not required to pay any Zakat (alms-tax).

In short Zakat becomes due and should be paid by the one's who have the worth of about 85 grams gold and more - and that it was with them for one complete year - and nothing was spent from it throughout the year!.

CHAPTER
9

HOW DID ISLAM BEGAN?

WHO CONVEYED THE MESSAGES OF ALLAH?:

By now readers would have acquired the general knowledge about the religion of Islam, the compulsory and voluntary rituals the followers of this religion have to perform, and the rules and conditions they have to adhere to. It will be proper now to know who conveyed these messages of Islam. And how it started to spread.

In the line of duty and to convey the heavenly messages of God, many prophets and messengers were chosen and selected to preach to their own people and society. Some of these messengers were not so lucky to their mission as their people failed them and did not listen to them, or did not obey the messages, and did not accept or follow these messengers. For example the people of Aad and Thamood or the people of Lott and Noah. Eventually those people were ceased and destroyed by the power of God when the earth was toppled for some or the floods drowned the others because of their bad deeds, aggression and inhuman and unnatural activities, and there was no good coming from them.

The messengers and prophets are sent among people to ask them to believe in God alone, and to advise them to do good among themselves and abstain from bad deeds and hurting others. Among the famous and most determined Prophets and Messangers of Allah in the later generations are Noah, Abraham Moses and Jesus (peace be upon them all) who conveyed the messages of God among their people.

HOW THE MESSAGES OF ISLAM CAME TO BE KNOWN?:

Prophet *Mohammad* (peace be upon him) was the last and final messenger and prophet of Allah, and on him the final messages were revealed to complete and compliment all the previously revealed heavenly and divine messages of God. He was chosen to be the messenger for all the people. As Allah mentioned in the Qur'an:

"And we have sent you thus, as kindness for all"

Mohammad (peace be upon him) conveyed all the message of Islam to all, As Islam is meant for all mankind.

HOW DID ISLAM BEGAN?:

At the time when *Mohammad* was born, the Arabian Peninsula was engulfed in the darkness of paganism - people were worshipping idols and deities of their own making. This era was known as the pagan era because of the ignorance among people, and the wild customs they used and adhere to. Among those customs was the burying alive of their new born or baby daughters. Some of them would feel ashamed if a baby girl was born in their family, and would burry their young daughters alive. Adultery and slavery were normal among them. There was no rule and regulations, (no law and order) or there were no state or Government as such to rule the people. It was tribal rules and the alliance was to the tribal chiefs, and the saying is for the strongest tribe.

During this Dark Age in history came the light of Islam shining when the revelations began and started being conveyed to the last and final messenger of God, *Mohammad* (peace be upon him). The first time the revelation came when he was in the Hira'a cave, and it continued to be reveled to him until he died in Madinah 23 years later. To know how Islam began we should read a short life-history or biography of Prophet *Mohammad* (peace be upon him) the messenger and Prophet of Islam, who was delegated the task of preaching and propagating Islam to all humanity. Because, Islam is not directed to one sect of people but it is meant for all. But here I will give a short account to the reader.

THE BEGINNING OF THE REVELATIONS OF ISLAM:

As a young man *Mohammad* was disturbed with the life concept of the people. They used to pray or worship the various idols which were erected or planted in and around the Kaabah; He did not like the pagan life and never followed or observed their customs. He used to think a lot, and started losing interest in his trade and business. The life of freedom as shepherds was not new for him - He used to leave Makkah and wander around, Later on he found a small cave in one of the small mountains around Makkah. It is called Mount Hira'a. He would stay in the Hira'a Cave for days meditating. His wife Lady Khadija saw him in this condition but did not stop or hindered his soul search. She used to make food and send it to him. She had a feeling that he was not behaving like this on his own. Something or some unknown force was behind his new behavior. So she helped him instead of depressing or discouraging him.

One day while he was meditating in this cave he was startled when a stranger suddenly appeared in front of him. He asked *Mohammad* to read. *Mohammad* answered him "What to read." *Mohammad* did not know how to read or write. The stranger embraced *Mohammad* strongly - until he was perspiring. The stranger then let loose of *Mohammad* and asked him again to read (or recite), to which *Mohammad* said "I am not reading", he did not know what to read, besides, there was nothing visible to read. The stranger again embraced *Mohammad* forcefully like before, and then let loose. And then asked him to recite after him".:

Read! In the Name of your Lord Who has created (all that exists)(1), He has created a man from a clot(2), Read! And your Lord is the Most Generous(3), Who has taught (the writing) by the pen(4), He has taught man that which he knew not(5). [96, Al-'Alaq]

Mohammad recited after him. The stranger then disappeared. This made *Mohammad* tremble in fear. He hurried back home. He asked that he be covered with a blanket. His wife Khadija was alarmed when she saw him trembling and sweating profusely. He told her about his encounter in the cave. She was a wise lady - she calmed him down and told him not to worry. She told him this could be the beginning of revelation's unto him. Because, she told him, he never did wrong or hurt anyone and he always kept in contact and never broke relations with his relatives. So he should not worry, that may be the beginning of a good sign, and a big mission awaited ahead of him.

Later on she took him along to her cousin warqa ibn Nowfal, who was an old priest and read all the divine books, she told her cousin of the encounter *Mohammad* had had in the cave. He confirmed her beliefs and told them that according to his knowledge the stranger could be the ArchAngel Gabriel who used to visit other prophets before him. He warned *Mohammad* that in the days to come his people would not like him and will put him to strong test and that they would try to hurt or harm him when he will tell them of the revelations he receives, and the new faith he is going to reveal unto them. This made *Mohammad* calm down his fear, and gave him the confidence that will make him anxious to have more encounters like this, with Archangel Gabriel.

This was the start of a new life for *Mohammad*. It was the beginning of a big change in the life of the people in Makkah and thereafter it will be a big and ominous change in the whole world. It was the beginning of the revelations of the light of Islam, which will enlighten the whole world with its teachings.

This was the beginning of a new life for *Mohammad* and his family. From now on there would be a big work to be done, a big responsibility to be shouldered and a big duty to be performed. The nights would be for praying and worship and the days would be to work hard and propagate the message of Islam, and even to fight for conveying this message. The people of Makkah used to like *Mohammad* until…. that day.

And that day arrived when those people stopped liking him. They instead were changing to became fierce enemies of the person they used to like. Because he started propagating a new religion, which is totally different from what they were believing in. They used to worship their many idols when *Mohammad* changed all that. His message was to stop this idol worshipping and instead believe in the oneness of God, Allah. They would not understand or agree and would not believe in his message. They did not like or want to leave what their fathers or forefathers used to worship. So, it was a new life for *Mohammad*, after he started receiving the revelations from Allah through His Arch Angel, Gabriel.

How did Islam spread:

In the beginning, Prophet *Mohammad* (Peace be upon him) received the first revelation through the Arch Angel Gabriel in the Hira Cave. The first person to which he told about this revelation was his wife Khadija. She knew about his honesty and that he never told lies, so she believed him whole heartedly. She comforted him, and in order to confirm it to him and to understand about the encounter *Mohammad* have had in the cave, she took him along to see her cousin Warqa ibn Noufal, who was an old priest who read the divine books, and who confirmed to them that it was the revelations which is being conferred on to *Mohammad* from God through His Arch Angel Gabriel.

Khadija, *Mohammad's* wife was the first person to believe in him. The second person was his close friend Abu Baker, who also without hesitance believed in him and in his new religion. And through him Othman also became a Muslim. The first among children was his cousin Ali ibn Abu Taleb. Slowly the circle of the believers in Islam started to become wide as the number of the believers increased but slowly. In the beginning they were in hiding, because the non believers of Makkah did not like them or their new faith. They used to like him until he started preaching the religion and faith of Islam.

They started to make life harder for *Mohammad*, his relatives, friends and followers. In some instances they used to severely punish and beat their own slaves or dependents who did accept and join the religion of Islam secretly.

The followers of *Mohammad* could not fight back because they were small in number. *Mohammad* would advise them to bear down the oppression. Omer was among the latest believers and who accepted Islam openly, and announced his change-over of his faith to the leaders of Quraish at the Kaabah and challenged them to stop or hinder him if they would dare. So basically Islam started from zero - until it became the fastest growing faith, and had one of the largest followers in the world.

Islam is a religion of peace and goodness, which it carries and propagates for humanity. Prophet *Mohammad* (peace be upon him) faced lots of difficulties and even the danger of being killed by the enemies of Islam. But he stood firm by his teachings.

He was safe among his people until his uncle Abu Taleb was alive. Because of his high position among the Quraish tribe of Makkah Abu Taleb was able to give protection to his nephew *Mohammad*. In one occasion the tribes in Makkah offered through his uncle to give *Mohammad* all the money and wealth if he wanted, or make him their ruler or leader if he so desires, in exchange or in return to that he would have to stop preaching or propagating his new faith and religion to the people in Makkah. This was a lucrative offer - which *Mohammad* refused. He said to his uncle, "even if they would put the sun in my right hand and the moon in my left hand and ask me to stop preaching for Islam I would not stop. Because it is the revelations from Allah that I am conveying to the people."

THE PLEDGE OF ALLEGIANCE OF AL OQABAH:

Life in Makkah become hard and unbearable for *Mohammad* and his followers. But far away in the city of Madinah people heard about the new Prophet and the new faith he was propagating in Makkah. They heard about him from the few pilgrims who returned back and who brought the news of the new religion being propagated in Makkah. Next year a team of twelve persons from Madinah visited Makkah. One night they met him at a designated place called AlOqbah, outside Makkah. They heard from him about his religion, and what it propagates, they were impressed and agreed to join Islam. They pledged allegiance to him and offered him to come to Madinah where they promised to help and give him shelter along with his followers. He sent with them an emissary Mosa'ab ibn Omair to the people in Madina to show them the teachings of Islam. The news about this new religion "Islam" spread readily among the people of Madinah. After spending some time in Madina Mosa'ab ibn Omair returned to Makkah, where he reported to the Prophet this good news, and also told him that more people from Madinah would be coming to meet him the coming year during their pilgrimage trip to Makkah.

The Prophet thought about the difference in attitude and good treatment his followers were getting in Madinah and the opposite situation of bad and severe treatment he and his followers were getting here in Makkah - big difference!

From here the idea and thinking was set to consider Madinah as his next step and platform for propagation. But the consent was yet to come from Allah for this migration, which eventually came.

That year (622AD) a big delegation of more than 600 persons came from Madinah. Among them were 75 persons, including two women, who already became Muslims, and all of them offered allegiance to the prophet and promised to protect him against his enemies with their lives if he came to live with them in Madinah.

This allegiance was known as the Great Bay'at Al Oqbah. And it was a turning point for good to the Muslims and Islam - And above all to the leader and mentor of Islam Prophet *Mohammad* (peace be upon him) who was invited to come to Madinah to make it his base with the promise to assist him and his followers fully against any aggression from anywhere.

It is appropriate now to know about prophet *Mohammad* (peace be upon him) who have conveyed the message of Islam and changed the course of history of human beings, and whom Allah have sent as blessings to the worlds.

CHAPTER 10

Prophet *MOHAMMAD*

(peace be upon him)

MOHAMMAD.. THE LAST PROPHET AND MESSENGER:

Mohammad (peace be upon him) was born in 570 AD. It was the year known in Arabia as the "year of the elephant" Because in that year Abraha the Ethiopian General who was appointed as Governor of Yemen came to Makkah on elephants, along with a big army to attack and destroy the Ka'abah, (the subject of this book).

Before *Mohammad* was born his father Abdullah bin Abdul Muttalib died. So he was born an orphan. After he was born, he was given to a Bedouin lady from Banu Sa'ad tribe to breast feed and take care of him. She was Haleema Al Saadiah. This was the norm in those days among the noble families of Makkah, to give their children among the Bedouin tribes, for care and up-bringing.

When he was young child, at the age of five, his mother Lady Amina bint Wahb also died on the way to Makkah after she left Yathreb (the old name of Madina). She went there to see her relatives, and also pay homage to her husband's grave. Abdullah ibn Abdul Muttaleb who was her husband and the father of *Mohammad* and who died there after a brief illness when he visited Yathreb shortly after their marriage. He was buried there, near Madina. So *Mohammad* was born and raised an orphan when his mother also died. This was a big tragedy for the small child *Mohammad*.

From now on he was taken care of by his grand father Abdul Muttalib who was well respected leader of the Quraish. When he was eight years old his grand father also died. He was as sad for the death of his grand father as he was when his mother died, because his grand father loved him very much and took good care of the young and orphaned *Mohammad*. His uncle Abu Taleb then took over the guardian ship, and so he was raised in the house hold of his uncle Abu Taleb. Abu Taleb was not very rich like *Mohammad's* other uncles, but even then he took good care of *Mohammad*, until he grew up to be a young man. From his childhood *Mohammad* was honest and trust worthy. He always spoke the truth.

COMMERCIAL/BUSINESS TRIPS:

At the age of twelve, *Mohammad* went on his first trip to the land of Syria. Syria was all those places which is now divided into many different countries which included Palestine, Jordon and Lebanon. Arab trade or commercial caravans used to travel from Makkah to Syria in the north during the summer time and to Yemen in the south during winter time where they used to bring goods and food to Makkah from these places and trade goods between these two far away places. Makkah became a commercial center at that time as well as being the religious center, because of the Kaabah in there. These commercial or trading trips are thus mentioned in the Qur'an:

106:1 FOR THE protection of Quraysh: their protection in their summer and winter Journeying. 106:2 Therefore let them worship the Lord of this House who fed them in the days of famine and shielded them from all peril.

So at the young age of twelve *Mohammad* wanted to go with his uncle Abu Taleb on one of those trips when he knew of his uncle's intention to join the caravan going to Syria. Because he knew and expected the dangers and hardship of such a long Journey, his uncle was reluctant to take him along. But when he saw the real desire of young *Mohammad* to accompany them, his uncle could not let him down and so he agreed, and took him along in this long journey. This trip was an experience for the young child *Mohammad*, who was amazed to see the vast lands of greenery in Syria, compared to the hard and dry land and the desert he came from. The trip was not very successful in trading for his uncle. And when they returned back to Makkah, his uncle did not plan to go again on another trip.

MOHAMMAD AS A SHEPHERD:

Mohammad spent many years of his youth taking care of the sheep and cattle he was herding in the valleys and mountains around Makkah. He joyously says of himself that he was a Sheppard like most of the prophets before him. He was shepherding the cattle of his uncle and other people of Makkah for a meager compensation - but he was content.

When he was in his teens and until the age of twenty he attended with his uncles and observed the wars of "Al Fujjar" between the Quraish tribe and other tribes around Makkah. In his twenties like in his youth he used to observe things and thinks a lot while he was sheparding or herding the cattle.

LADY KHADIJA:

His uncle Abu Talib was not very rich person and he had many children of his own. He wanted to help , and when he heard that one of the rich ladies of Makkah was looking for an agent for her trading business, to go on the caravan to Syria, he asked *Mohammad* if he would like to go on this trip. *Mohammad* liked the idea and agreed. Abu Taleb, who was a respectable Quraish leader, talked to her. She was Khadija bint Khwailed, the well known noble and rich lady in Makkah. He told her about his nephew *Mohammad* and if she would take him to be her agent for this trading trip. Because she, like the others in Makkah, had heard about his honesty and knew that he was trust worthy, she readily agreed and appointed him as her agent to take care of her business interests on the trip.

When the caravan arrived in Syria he did great trading and made good profit and bought lots of goods which Lady Kahdija had asked for. This was the first time she made a good profit in her trade. She was impressed with the young man whom she entrusted her riches with. Her servant "Maysara'" also told her of the honest way *Mohammad* was doing business in this trip. Because she heard so much about him and of his honesty and charm, Khadija could not but admire and respect *Mohammad.*

She was a rich and noble lady and many a rich suitors had proposed to marry her before, but she did refuse them. She was forty years old then, and *Mohammad* was twenty-five. He did not even think about this when she offered to marry him. He agreed and went to his uncle Abu Taleb, and told him about her proposal and that he agreed to marry her.

Even at that time and before the advent of Islam, people in Makkah had a respect for custom and tradition. So his uncles and relatives went with him to Khadija's uncle and asked him for the marriage of Khadija to *Mohammad* - and so they were married. For the lonely *Mohamma*d this was a new life of Marriage and comfort.

MOHAMMAD AS A FATHER:

Lady Khadija loved *Mohammad* as her husband and took good care of him. During their marriage, they had many children. Two sons Al Qasim and Abdullah, and four daughters Zainab, Ruqayah, Om Kulthoum and Fatima. His sons died when they were young. *Mohammad* was very sad for the death of his young sons but accepted the will of God. They were born before the revelations that he became the Prophet of Allah, and before his migration to Madinah.

Many years later in Madinah and while he was burying his youngest son Ibrahim who was born in Madinah from another wife, and who died there, Prophet *Mohammad* (peace be upon him) said with tears in his eyes, "we are very sad for your departure O Ibrahim, but we cannot say anything except what pleases Allah", and then he read the verse from Qur'an?

(We all belong to Allah and to Him we return.)

WHY DOES SOLAR AND LUNAR ECLIPSE HAPPENS?!:

Prophet *Mohammad* was never a pretender or claimant of wrong or false assumptions. After his young son Ibrahim died, a solar eclipse happened. Some people and followers said the sun eclipsed because of the death of the Prophet's son. They said that the Sun was sad because of the death of Ibrahim. He did not let the sayings of the people go without answer or, showing them the right path. He did not concur or confirm their sayings even by keeping quite about the matter.

When the eclipse happened, the Prophet hurriedly left his house and entered the mosque with his followers and called for prayers. When people gathered in the mosque he began praying and worshipping Allah, until the eclipse passed away. After the prayers he climbed the pulpit and addressed the people after praising and thanking Allah and said which means that,: "The sun and the moon are signs of the marvels of Allah. They do not become eclipsed because of the death or birth of anyone. When it happens, you should go to your prayers and ask Allah for forgiveness, until it passes away. It is the way God has made the universe and the planets in it, and made its ways of movements".

In the later days many things were found by scientists about this phenomena and now we know more about the solar system and how the eclipse happens. When the moon in its rotations comes in between the sun and the earth, and blocks the sun causing it to hide behind the moon, it is called (the solar) eclipse. And when the earth in its movements comes in between the moon and the sun it blocks the sun light to the moon and the moon is fully or partially hidden by the earth and becomes dark, that is called moon (or lunar) eclipse.

THE PROPHET'S NOCTURNAL JOURNEY:

The Prophet's nocturnal (midnight) journey to al Aqsa Mosque (in Jerusalem) and his ascension to the seventh heaven. This is one of the many miracles, which had happened during his lifetime, and it was the most important aspect in the life of Prophet *Mohammad*, after the revelations of the Qur'an he began receiving at the Hira'a cave.

As mentioned before, in the beginning of his propagation of Islam Prophet *Mohammad* (peace be upon him) was met with strong resistance for his message and religion. Instead of accepting his call, most of his acquaintance and friends refused it and became his ardent enemies, especially after the death of his uncle Abu Taleb, who was providing him with the well required support and protection he needed, from his enemies. Shortly there after the death of his wife Lady Khadija who used to be his kind supporter and comforter. Now he had no one to turn to for help when needed.

One night while he was unhappy and depressed because of the ill treatment he was getting from the people in Makkah, Prophet *Mohammad* was taken to a life-time journey which opened the whole universe for him to see, when he was flown from Makkah to the Al Aqsa Mosque where he prayed two raka'ats. From there he was raised to heaven with the Arch Angel Gabriel accompanying him He was raised to the 1st heaven or sky, and then he ascended to the 2nd, 3rd, until he was at the 7th heaven (or sky). From there he was taken to the final boundary of heavens (beyond which no one could pass). There is the lote tree The Sidrat Al Muntaha, where he was bestowed-upon the salat rituals five times a day which was to be conveyed to his disciples or followers of Islam to perform. He was also shown a glimpse of the destiny of the people, and how will they be in heavens or hell, according to their beliefs and deeds in this world. He also met some of the earlier messengers and prophets in each of those seven heavens. Then he was descended down and taken back to Makkah. All in a one night journey. A detailed description of this exalted and exciting journey could be found in many of the life history of Prophet *Mohammad* (peace be upon him) and in the interpretation of the Holy Qur'an.

Next day he told about this trip to Abu-Jahal, a Quraish leader, who became an ardent enemy of *Mohammad* (peace be upon him), who made fun of this account and mockingly called on the people to listen to this "amazing" story from *Mohammad*. Many of them were really amazed, especially when he vividly described all of the Al Aqsa mosque when he was asked to do so, and also the familiar marks he saw on the way to Jerusalem. But most of them did not accept this venture and thought it to be an imagination.

The only person among those people who accepted this narration of *Mohammad* (peace be upon him) and believed it without reluctance was his friend Abu Bakr. Who when told about this miraculous adventure, said "If *Mohammad* said it, than it is true."

After this journey Arch Angel Gabriel visited Prophet *Mohammad* (peace be upon him) and he showed him how to offer the prayers and consequently he would come and show him all the prayers, and how it is done in its proper timings.

THE EXODUS TO MADINAH:

Because of the hardship and torments the believers received at the hands of their enemies in Makkah, many of them fled to Ethiopia - where they were accepted and protected by the kind and just King at that time in Ethiopia - King Najashi.

But after some time many of these migrants returned back to Makkah, and when they knew that the Prophet gave his consent for his followers to migrate to Madinah, the Muslims started for this new exodus. The increasing number of Muslims migrating to Madinah made the unbelievers in Makkah fear for the unknown.

So they put a strong resistance to stop this increasing flow of exodus to Madinah. Many of the migrating people had to pay as ransom their houses, and in some cases give all their belongings so as to be able to leave Makkah, safely.

MOHAMMAD'S (PEACE BE UPON HIM) MIGRATION TO MADINAH (622 AD – 12 RABIE I) :

People in Makkah used to like him and called him Al Ameen (the trust worthy) until he started preaching for the new religion of Islam! There after they became his ardent enemies. And the biggest fear and concern of the unbelievers was that *Mohammad* may also leave Makkah and will find a strong base in Madinah. Because they found out that the people in Madinah were joining this new religion in great numbers. To stop this influx to Madinah they conspired to kill *Mohammad*. And to avoid having to put the blame on a single tribe and face a war alone with Bani Hashem sect of the Quraish tribe or having to pay the blood money alone they decided to spread the crime and consequence on all the tribes. They agreed that a member of each tribe will join and gather to attack *Mohammad* jointly all together kill him. This way the Bani Hashem sect to whom *Mohammad* belonged would not be able to fight all the tribes to avenge his death. And they would have to accept the blood money which will be spread between them all, and it becomes very little for each tribe to pay. What a satanic idea!.

Allah revealed to his Prophet *Mohamma*d about this conspiracy. It was difficult and dangerous for him now to stay in Makkah so the consent was granted to *Mohammad* to leave Makkah for Madinah. The young warriors from each tribe surrounded the Prophets house as vigilantes and took turn for this vigilance so that *Mohammad* would not slip-by from them.

Prophet *Mohamma*d asked his cousin Ali ibn Abu Taleb to take his place in his bed that night as a camouflage. He was sure they would not kill Ali because he was not the one they were after. Next morning the vigilantes were surprised to see Ali wakes up from Prophet *Mohammad's* bed. They knew then that the Prophet has slipped by them the previous night – while they were supposed to be on alert and on the watch.

Before migrating Prophet *Mohammad* had left with Ali all the trusts which were entrusted and deposited in his care and were kept in his custody, with instructions to give it back to its owners before he himself could leave Makkah and follow them later to Madinah. He had earlier told his friend Abu Bakr to stay ready for departure and become his companion in the upcoming journey. And together they would leave Makkah.

That night and before dawn Prophet *Mohammad* left his house. He saw all those young vigilantes were fast asleep as he passed besides them. He went to Abu Bakr's house who was also ready to leave on a short notice, with the prophet. They immediately went out of Makkah towards the south instead of going towards Madinah in the north to deceive their enemies. They went to a cave called "Thor" and stayed there in order that the search parties after them will stop or slow down when in the morning they will find him missing and departed. The prophet and his companion and close friend Abu Bakr stayed there in the "Thor cave" for three days. During their stay in the cave the search party looking for them even passed by the cave door but did not see them. After the 3rd day they slipped out of the cave and began their travel along with a guide who knows the way to Madinah, where they arrived several days later, after an adventurous trip, which by itself was a great miracle. And there he was accorded a warm welcome.

BOUNTY HUNTERS:

To foil his escape the Quraish leaders set a reward of 100 mature camels to whoever would catch *Mohammad* dead or alive. This set the greed' in many people who became the bounty hunters. Among them Suraqa who after several days of tracking found the Prophet and his companion Abu Bakr. But he was not able to reach them, as his horse would tumble and fall every time he tried to get near them. This was also among the many miracles which happened to the Prophet. He realized then that there is a divine force which was protecting the Prophet and his companion. Finally he gave up his efforts and asked the Prophet's forgiveness and went back to Makkah. He was given promise by the Prophet that he will be rewarded or compensated later on, when he comes to Madinah. Later on, he became a Muslim and came to Madinah.

After the death of the Prophet he did receive the reward which the Prophet had promised him to receive, from the bounties which came from Persia at the time of the 2nd Caliph Omar ibn Al Khattab.

PROPHET *MOHAMMAD'S* ARRIVAL IN MADINAH.

Prophet *Mohammad* (peace be upon him) and his friend and companion Abu-Bakr arrived in Quba'a at the outskirt of Madinah on the 2nd of Rabea I which correspond to 20 Sept. 622 AD. From this period starts the Islamic calendar which is depicted with the symbol (AH) After Hijrah, which means (after date of migration).

Contrary to the mistreatment he was subjected to, and refusal of his messages by his own people in his birth place, Makkah, the people of Madinah were waiting eagerly to receive him, as they heard about him and his message, and many of them have already accepted Islam and became Muslims. Since they knew of his departure from Makkah they would watch and await his arrival every day.

They were very happy the day he arrived at Quba'a and all the people including women and children came to welcome him warmly. It was a day of celebration and festivity for all. He stayed in Quba'a for few days where he built the first Mosque built in Islam.

During the last (12) twelve years *Mohammad* and his companions were literally abandoned and oppressed in Makkah. They could not do any of their rites or rituals openly.

But here in Madinah it became totally different when the Mosque for prayers was built in the Quba'a area, and the second Mosque was built in proper Medinah (or the city center) where the Prophet of

Islam built his house and built the mosque besides it.

The people of Madinah joined and accepted Islam whole-heartedly and so there were many mosques built in a short time so that prayers could be performed openly and in congregations.

The city of Madinah was the refuge and shelter for Prophet *Mohamma*d (peace be upon him) his companions, disciples and followers of Islam. In a while it became also the capital of Islamic state and people from all over world visit it, to see and meet the Prophet in there. Even emissaries and ambassador from far away places will come to visit him – in his mosque.

Prophet *Mohammad* (peace be upon him) became the ultimate ruler of the hearts and minds of the people besides being the actual ruler of a newly built state of Islam.

Even with all the worldly power and position he had, Prophet *Mohammad* never sought or desired to indulge in the worldly pomp and prestige which other rulers would yearn for. He still lived in a simple house built by mud and clay and lived a simple life throughout his life.

MUHAJREEN AND ANSARS:

After settling down in Madinah *Mohammad* (peace be upon him) and his followers made it their base and the Capital of their faith, which he solidified with the ever increasing number of followers who became Muslims.

The people in Madinah now became two known factions. The Muhajreen (or the Migrants) and the Ansar (The patrons or allies). The Ansar's are the original citizens of Madinah. When the Muhajreen or migrants came flowing into Madinah from Makkah, the Ansars of Madinah received them well and welcomed them greatly. And when the Prophet came to Madina he strengthened the relation's between these two factions and made it a brotherly relation between them. The Ansars of Madinah shared their houses and business with them, and offered half of their belongings to the Muhajreen who came into Madinah poor and empty handed as they had to leave their houses and all their belongings in Makkah as ransom, fleeing from the oppression they had encountered and faced from the unbelievers of Quraish in Makkah. The Prophet liked the Ansar's and have emphasized to all to treat them well in his farewell speech in Arafat. This was in recognition and gratefulness for their generosity and hospitality they extended to him, his companions and followers the Muhajreen (immigrants) when they arrived bare handed and poor - fleeing from the aggressors in Makkah.

THE INCURSIONS:

After solidifying his base in Madinah the Prophet and his followers had many incursions in and around Madinah. Some of these incursions were invasions to deter an attack, and some were for defense. Also it was time to gain strength and self confidence.

Example: When the news came that Abu Sufyan a great Quraish leader was leading a big trading caravan from Makkah to Syria this made the Muhajreen think of invading this caravan and obtain what it was carrying. That was in revenge of what they suffered physically, materially and financially at the hands of Quraish before leaving Makkah. The Prophet agreed with them and sent a cavalry to intercept the caravan. Abu Sufyan came to know about this, he hurriedly changed course and evaded the incursion. At the same time he sent a message to Quraish leaders in Makkah, informing them about it, and asked for help to meet and protect him and his caravan on the way back, when he comes from Syria.

THE BATTLE OF BADR:

The leaders of Quraish in Makkah were agitated with this news and prepared an army of thousand strong ones to come and protect this caravan as it contains valuables for most of the people in Makkah.

On the way back Abu Sufyan did evade the incursion again and was on his way to Makkah, where he arrived safely. He sent a message to Abu Jahl an uncle of the Prophet who was leading the Quraish army that every thing was OK and well and that he and his army could return back to Makkah. But Abu Jahl ignored this message and vowed that he would be happy and will enjoy killing *Mohammad* and his followers.

The news of this army came to the Prophet and it was decided to meet this army away from Madinah. This was a strategic decision. He along with about three hundred of his followers left Madinah. It was a small force and inadequately equipped compared to Abu Lahab's well equipped force which consist of cavalries and camel riders besides the ones on foot. They camped in a place called Badr about 70 miles south west of Madinah.

The two forces met in Badr during the month of Ramadan (17th). One army was large and well equipped force, but without faith, from Makkah. And the other was a small number of people poorly equipped, but spiritually confident, from Madinah. After a fierce fighting where the infidels from Makkah lost many of their members in the battle, they retreated. This was the first large incursion or fight the Muslims encountered and they were successful. This was known as the incursion of Badr.

BATTLE OF OHOD:

After suffering this defeat the infidels of Makkah were angered - and they vowed to revenge. Next year they gathered larger number of force of about 3000 persons and started towards Madinah. The news came to Prophet *Mohammad*. He also started preparing his army and with a force of about 1000 people he set out of Madinah to meet the invaders. They met out side Madinah at a place called OHOD. In the beginning and after a fierce fight the Muslims were successful and the Quraish army started retreating and fleeing back.

But because of the untimely jubilation of their victory and the dis-obedience of his order by some of his troops, the Muslims suffered great losses and their victory turned into asorrow retreat..The sharp shooters who were placed strategically over OHOD mountain and were instructed to cover the Muslim army from behind. They had their orders not to leave their positions regardless of any way the fight turns. Some of them seeing the enemy fleeing thought the war was over, and ran into the battle field to grab some of the spoils of the retreating army of Quraish.

The army of *Mohammad* (peace be upon him) suffered a great loss by this un-acceptable action and disobedience leaving their strategic positions opened.

Seeing this great chance the enemy regrouped and attacked them from behind as the Muslim sharp shooters left their position disobey-ing the clear instructions of the prophet and the strategic position was left open.

The Muslims fought back until the invaders gave up the fight and retreated towards Makkah. In this fight a close friend and uncle of the Prophet, Hamza ibn Abdal Muttaleb, was killed and his body was mutilated by Hind, the wife of Abu Sufyan a leader of Quraish, in revenge of her sons who were killed in the earlier battle of Badr. This made the Prophet sad for his uncle's death, but as usual in all his losses and ordeals he accepted the will of God.

This way the Muslims and faithfuls had gained experience of warfare, and the confidence to fight any invaders, and gained the faith that makes them conquer any army, and bear or endure any hardships, and to adhere to the instructions they receive.

MOHAMMAD'S ARDENT ENEMIES:

Some readers would be wondering why Prophet *Mohammad's* uncle was fighting against him instead of being his allied, and support him. Well - he had many uncles - but only one of them became his ardent and fiercest enemy. He was Abu Lahab (Abdul Ozza bin Abd Al Muttaleb) who was mentioned in Surat (Al Masad - 111) in the Qur'an. The other fierce enemy was Abu Jahal (Omr bin Hisham bin Al Moghaira) a young Quraish leader from Banu Makhzoum sect and not from the Banu Hashim sect like the Prophet.

They became enemies because of two reasons the foremost of it is jealousy. Jealousy is the worst self inflicted mental illness anyone could encounter. It is a killer disease which finishes the one who carries it., before it could destroy the one's a person may have grudge against.

So it was jealousy against *Mohammad* by these two great leaders of Quraish. One was the chief of the Quraish tribe and as all attention and lime-light was diverted from him since the prophet announced his mission after receiving the revelations. And the other was his uncle who was of the opinion or dream that the revelations should have been bestowed on him and not on his nephew, as he was the patriarch of the family. They did not reason to themselves that Allah will bestow His blessings to whom ever He chooses and not according to anyone's dreams or wishes, and that no one has the right to question His judgment and prerogative. He is the Lord and the best of Judges.

PROPHET *MOHAMMAD'S* STRONG SUPPORTERS:

Contrary to his uncle Abu Lahab who suddenly became one of his archenemies after he started propagating Islam, there were also his other uncles who loved and supported him strongly.

His uncle Abu Talib who became Prophet *Mohammad's* guardian and portege after his grand father Abdul Muthalib's death.

Abu Talib took care of *Mohammad* since he was young and became his protector and protege since he started his mission until he died but unfortunately without becoming a Muslim. His other uncle Hamza became his friend and strong supporter after he embraced Islam. He was non-muslim one day he knew that Abu Jahal mocked *Mohammad* and insulted him openly. Hamza bin Abdul Muthalib became furiously angry and went to Abu Jahal's house and insulted him strongly in response to his attack on *Mohammad*. He was not a Muslim then. But after this incident he announced his admission in Islam, and became one of the strong helper and supporter of Prophet *Mohammad* (peace be upon him).

He Joined prophet in his battle of Ohod againts the infidels who came from Makkah to revenge their defeat in the battle of Badr. Hamza was killed in support of Islam in the battle of Ohod. The prophet was very sad at Hamza's death and Hamza was buried in Madinah at the base of Ohod Mountain.

THE REASONS BEHIND THE INCURSIONS:

Besides the battles of Badr and Ohod the Muslims had many incursions of offence and defense between themselves and the many tribes in Arabia. In all the circumstances the outcome was good and favourable as the numbers of the believers were increasing - always, as many of the fighting enemy soldiers would join the side of *Mohammad* and become Muslims.

To alleviate the misunderstanding and misconception of many - it is important to emphasize a simple logic in the propagation of any faith or religion. No one could be compelled deep inside, to change or convert into something he would not accept or believe in whole heartedly, and for the rest of his life! It is the matter of reaching a person and delivering the message - and the outcome would be his own decision. Muslims in the beginning had to fight to defend themselves to survive.

Secondly they had to fight to strengthen their power so as not to be bothered again and again. Sometimes they had to wage war so as to stop being attacked. The first few years Muslims in Madinah had to fight their way to strengthen their base and as such there were many battles they fought.

In the 6th year after migration, Prophet *Mohammad* decided to go to Makkah to perform Omra. He took with him several hundreds of his companions and followers. The Quraish heard about his travel to Makkah. They feared that he was coming to attack them. So they gathered thousands of their army to meet *Mohammad* (peace be upon him) and his companions.

WHAT IS JIHAD OR (INCURSION):

Islam began as a weak entity. It started when the revelations began to arrive to Prophet *Mohammad* (peace be upon him). Then few of his relatives and acquaintance accepted Islam without reluctance. First among these pioneers was his wife Lady Khadija - his friend Abu Bakr and his cousin Ali, who was a child then. This small number started to increase slowly and steadily. In the course of period of more than ten years in Makkah the small numbers of Muslims were treated badly and aggressively, which they had to bear down. This was a silent struggle or Jihad for survival.

After migration to Madinah (622 AD) their numbers started to increase rapidly, as the people of Madinah who became known as the "Ansars" or the Protégées, started joining this religion in greater numbers, which made their enemies in Makkah rage in anger and envy. So they planned to attack them in Madinah. And to fight back in defense for survival became a continuous struggle or Jihad, which the Prophet had to do in defense of this religion and its followers, and also to strengthen it against its enemies and deter them.

To defend themselves Muslims had to fight, this war is called Jihad, mostly in defense. But sometimes they had to be on the offensive to deter or scare their enemies. It is like a military strategy. In all these wars and incursions Muslims are encouraged to defend their religion without being afraid to die as their cause of fight is noble and so the ones who die in this cause are awarded the title of martyrs and raised to heavens, and are promised a higher place in Paradise, by Allah.

Also the ones who avoid to join the forces for Jihad or to fight the wars against the enemies of Islam are promised the wrath and the displeasure of Allah. Because to defend your religion, your-self, your family and dignity, and your country are among the noble causes to fight for and go on the Jihad.

Jihad is a sacred form of worship which Muslims or the believers would not avoid when confronted with, by their enemies. Jihad means to raise high the sign of the one-ness of Allah. Jihad is to fight for the cause of Islam and raising its banner high among nations, and in defense of its followers and disciples. Jihad is derived from the word Johd, which means struggle. It is a struggle for survival. Muslims would not desire or wish for war, but when confronted with it they should defend themselves and should not turn back to flee.

Like any other religion or faith, Muslims will fight to defend their religion and faith, to the end. Jihad is to uphold and raise the command of Allah, and to defend the faith of Islam. In it Muslims have many forms to defend their faith, and themselves. Foremost of it is to join the Muslim army in war and participate personally - No escape from duty or draft avoidance!

The second form of Jihad is to participate also financially when you have the means to do so if and when required. In the beginning of Islam when the Muslim army was ill-equipped because of short of funds, The Prophet asked his companions and followers to help in this cause with financial contributions.

Every one did according to their ability and means. And the most famous among them was Othman ibn Affan, the famous companion who later became the third Caliph, and Abdul Rahman ibn Oaf another famous and wealthy companion, who on many occasions did help to fully equip the army from their personal resources and contributions when it was going for Jihad.

140

The prophet's companions would compete with each other to give and contribute voluntarily whatever they had in their means and possessions, whenever situation arose. Foremost of them are Abu Bakr and Also Omer, the second Caliph of The Prophet besides the two mentioned above. Islam avoids war and aggression, but does not accept oppression, and Muslims would not avoid going for Jihad when forced or confronted by its enemies.

The Prophet would use civil methods of diplomatic talks and reasoning before being forced into war, and then Jihad is the final alternative. The year before entering Makkah, The Prophet had the peace agreement of Hodaibia with Quraish leaders who reneged from this agreement and thus Jihad was the unavoidable solution, and The Prophet entered Makkah triumphantly in the 8th year after migration, - (630 AD) without war or blood-shed.

THE TREATY OF HODAIBIA:

In the 6th year after the migration (AH), the Prophet (peace be upon him) wanted to perform Omra in Makkah. He announced his wish to his companions and followers in Madinah and prepared for this journey. Hundreds of his followers followed him in this journey. When he arrived at Hodaibia a place outside Makkah, he put his camp. He sent his emissaries under the leadership of Othman ibn Affan to Makkah to advise them of his peaceful intention of doing the Omra. The people of Makkah were relieved that *Mohammad* did not come to attack them. Even then, they refused him to do the Omra this year. The leaders of Quraish were putting up face with their own people in Makkah. And they demanded that *Mohammad* (peace be upon him) should return back to Madinah for the time being. But they would agree for him to come to Makkah next year, when they will allow him to stay for three days to perform the rituals around the Ka'abah. Despite the reluctance of some of his companions, *Mohammad* (peace be upon him) accepted this agreement - which eventually was to change the history of Islam, and he agreed to return back to Madinah without performing the Omra. This treaty was the basis for the full recognition of the prophet of Allah as a state leader, by the non believers of Makkah.

The next year prophet *Mohammad* (peace be upon him) along with about 1500 of his followers prepared to go to Makkah to do the Omra as it was agreed. They took their arms with them, just in case. He did not wanted to be taken by surprise in Makkah. When they arrived in Makkah they entered the Haram without their arms - they made groups, a group would stay out side the Haram, keeping their arms ready - and guarding the arms of the group who are inside the Haram. When they completed their rituals, *Mohammad* (peace be upon him) and his party peacefully left Makkah and returned back to Madinah, as agreed the previous year in the treaty.

THE CONQUEST OF MAKKAH (8TH YEAR AH – 630 AD) RAMADAN:

Mohammad (peace be upon him) was bound by the treaty of Hudaibiya - not to wage war unless any of the group annuls this treaty by attacking the other side or their allies.

Prophet *Mohammad* (peace be upon him) adhered to the treaty but Quraish did not. They aided their allies from Banu Bakr and killed about 20 of *Mohammad's* (Peace be upon him) allies. His allies the Khuza'as sent a message for help.

After the killings Quraish realized the blunder they did. They hurriedly sent Abu Sufian as their emissary to dissuade *Mohammad* from waging war onto Makkah. It was too late because *Mohammad* (peace be upon him) had already promised his allies to help them and prepared his army to March on to Makkah. He and his army Marched secretly to Makkah. He did not want to have full fledged war. He arrived in Makkah and took it and its people by surprise. When he entered Makkah he announced that whoever took refuge at Abu Sufyan's house (Quraish leader who had joined Islam) or stayed at his own house and would not fight, would be safe. It was the biggest victory so far to the Muslims.

After attaining the big victory in Makkah He gathered the people of Makkah and the Quraish leaders. They were in thousands. He asked them what they would expect him now to be doing with them – They said to him you are generous and merciful brother, and we expect your forgiveness. To which he said God will forgive you and you are free to leave. They all gave him the pledge of allegiance.

Mohammad (peace be upon him) knew that by controlling the Quraish of Makkah he basically and strategically controlled most of the Arabian tribes in the Arabian peninsula - except for the few who within the next few years had joined *Mohammad* (peace be upon him) and his group.

After the conquest of Makkah without a big fight, and because of his lenient attitude towards his old enemies - *Mohammad* captured the hearts of the people in Makkah. They flocked in large numbers to pay homage to him, and to pledge allegiance. The people of Makkah who were his ardent enemies happily became Muslims. In the next few days he removed and destroyed all the deities and idols from in and around the Ka'abah. He asked Bilal to climb on top of the Kaabah and announce the call for the prayers. The conquest of Makkah was the turning point for Islam. It confirmed and firmly laid the foundation and the state hood of Islam – on the Arabian Peninsula, and it was the great achievement for Prophet *Mohammad* (peace be upon him).

After the conquest of Makkah and the big victory he had, Prophet *Mohammad* (peace be upon him) returned back to Madinah.

In the next couple of years he solidified his base and united the whole of the Arabian Peninsula. Madinah then was recognized as base or capital of the Muslim state.

In the 10th AH year Prophet *Mohammad* (peace be upon him) went to Makkah to perform Hajj, and there he had the notion, and he knew that he is not going to live longer, when he received the last revelation of the Qura'an, among which it was thus mentioned:

"This day I have perfected for you your religion and completed my favour unto you, and choosen Islam for you as your religion."{ 5:03}

After completing performance of Hajj he returned back to Madinah. And in the same year 11th (AH) (8th June, 632 AD), the Prophet of Islam died in Madinah after a short illness He was buried in his own house which was adjacent to the Mosque he built in Madinah, when he arrived there migrating from Makkah eleven years ago.

PROPHET *MOHAMMAD'S* LIFE IN MADINAH:

Prophet *Mohammad* (peace be upon him) spent the last 11 years of his life in Madinah, propagating and teaching the lessons of Islam.

Madinah became the center or Capital of the Islamic State during his time and Islam has spread throughout the Arabian Peninsula and the neighbor hood. He became the social and political leader besides the religious responsibilities he performed. Hence, all these responsibilities are inter-related because most of the social or political norms or activities are based on the religious and spiritual values - and thus in Islam state and religion are not separate entity.

Prophet *Mohammad* was in practical sense the ruler in his time. He ruled over the hearts and minds of the people before their bodies. His wishes were their command - and they loved him dearly more than themselves, their parents or their own children, and they obey all what he says, and follows what he did. After 14 centuries from when he started teaching and preaching the lessons of Islam, Prophet *Mohammad* (peace be upon him) still command the same love respect and reverence by his Muslim followers through out the world.

He lived the life of piety and nobleness. He did not build palaces for himself or for his family and friends. He would hold council, decides the affair of the people and the state - from that holy place the mosque he built besides his own house. And also he would meet the emissaries, ambassadors and foreign dignitaries coming from all around the world in there, and his companions would assist him in his daily tasks or whatever he asks them to do. He lived a simple life and he was very generous in giving whatever he receives as gifts, to the needy and the poor, leaving nothing for himself and his family and friends. They also accepted happily this simple life and situation without hesitation and were contented.

PROPHET *MOHAMMAD'S* DEATH: (MON 12 RABIE' AWAL 11 AH) (8th June 632 AD):

Not very long after Prophet *Mohammad* (peace be upon him) arrived back in Madinah - after performing Hajj he felt sick. He started getting headache which would sometimes become severe - Later on he had fever. Even though he was sick he still would lead the congregational prayers in the mosque which he had built adjacent to his house. His illness extended to several days (about two weeks) until he was not able to lead the prayers in the last couple of days before his death as he became very weak, and the illness and fever became severe. He ordered that his close friend and sincere companion Abu Bakr should lead the prayers. At one time when he felt he could enter the mosque he did- and he did ask Abu Bakr to continue leading the congregation while the prophet offered his prayers sitting on the right side of Abu Bakr, because he was too weak to offer his prayers standing. Even in the last days of his life the prophet was teaching the believers not to go astray from prayers as it is one of the fundamental pillars of Islam and Muslims have to offer their prayers even if they are very ill - or in their sick bed. And the Prophet of Islam *Mohammad* (peace be upon him) died in Madinah in the 11th Year AH at the age of 63.

He conveyed the messages of Islam by his sayings, and deeds tire-lessly relentlessly, honestly and truthfully from when he started receiving the revelations until the last day in his life. And as being described in the Qur'an he was sent by God as a blessing to all humanity in this world. So when he died in 632 AD Madinah became a sad city for a long time - until his pious successors or caliph Rashedeen could eleviate this sadness with their sincere follow-up of the prophet's foot steps.

PROPHET *MOHAMMAD'S* PERSONALITY (PEACE BE UPON HIM):

Here is a condensed recollection, a kind of verbal icon, of that Prophetic beauty. It is paraphrased from a passage by Imam al-Ghazali, in Book 19 of his Revival of the Religious Sciences, Ihya Ulum al-Din:

'The Messenger of God (s) was the mildest of men, but also the bravest and most just of men. He was the most restrained of people; never touching the hand of a woman over whom he did not have rights, or who was not his mahram. He was the most generous of men, so that never did a gold or silver coin spend the night in his house. If something remained at the end of the day, because he had not found someone to give it to, and night descended, he would go out, and not return home until he had given it to someone in need. From what Allah gave him, he would take only the simplest and easiest foods: dates and barley, giving anything else away in the path of Allah. Never did he refuse a gift for which he was asked. He used to mend his own sandals, and patch his own clothes, and serve his family, and help them to cut meat. He was the shyest of men, so that his gaze would never remain long in the face of anyone else. He would accept the invitation of a freeman or a slave, and accept a gift, even if it were no more than a gulp of milk, or the thigh of a rabbit, and offer something in return. He never consumed anything given in sadaqa. He was not too proud to reply to a slave, or a pauper in rags. He would become angered for his Lord, never for himself; he would cause truth and justice to prevail even if this led to discomfort to himself or to his companions. He used to bind a stone around his waist out of hunger. He would eat what was brought, and would not refuse any permissible food. If there were dates without bread, he would eat, if there was rough barley bread, if there was only yogurt, he would be quite satisfied with that. He was not sated, even with barley-bread, for three consecutive days, until the day he met his Lord, not because of poverty, or avarice, but because he was contented.

'He would attend weddings, and visit the sick, and attend funerals, and would often walk among his enemies without a guard. He was the most humble of men, and the most serene, without arrogance. He was the most eloquent of men, without ever speaking for too long. He was the most cheerful of men. He was afraid of nothing in this world. He would wear a rough Yemeni cloak, or a woolen tunic; whatever was lawful and was to hand, that he would wear. He would ride whatever was to hand: sometimes a horse, sometimes a camel, sometimes a mule, sometimes a donkey. And at times he would walk, without head cover or a turban or a cap. He would visit the sick even if they were in the farthest part of Madina. He loved perfumes, and disliked foul smells.

'He maintained affectionate and loyal ties with his relatives, but without preferring them to anyone who was superior to them. He never snubbed anyone. He accepted the excuse of anyone who made an excuse. He would joke, but would never say anything that was not true. He would laugh, but not uproariously. He would watch permissible games and sports, and would not criticize them. He ran races with his wives. Voices would be raised around him, and he would be patient. He kept a goat, from which he would draw milk for his family. He would walk among the fields of his companions. He never despised any pauper for his poverty or illness; neither did he hold any king in awe simply because he was a king. He would call rich and poor to Allah, without distinction.

'In him, Allah combined all noble traits of character; although he neither read nor wrote, having grown up in a land of ignorance and deserts in poverty, as a shepherd, and as an orphan with neither father nor mother. But Allah Himself taught him all the excellent qualities of character, and praiseworthy ways, and the stories of the early and the later prophets, and the way to salvation and triumph in the after world (here - in - after), and to joy and detachment in the this world, and how to hold fast to duty.

CHAPTER 11

CALIPHATES AND SCHOLARS

AL KHALIFAH (CALIPHATE):

There were many great companions of the Prophet during his lifetime. They were honest, sincere and faithful companions.

They stood fast and fought with him. They gave full support to all his calls and decisions. They were ready to give their life for the religion and faith they accepted and agreed to sincerely. Among those companions, there were four of Prophet *Mohammad's* (peace be upon him) close friends and followers, who took charge of the newly established Islamic state, and the Muslims affairs as the Khalifa's or the Poise Successors after his death.

They cemented and expanded the bases and realm of Islam in far away places during their time, through their farsighted vision, selfless endeavors, honesty and hard work. They expanded the call of Islam through vast places and land through their wise and exemplary rule. In their time the ways and means of proper Government machinery were devised, law and justice were the supreme order of their government. They did not appoint their own friends and relatives in important positions or Jobs. They appointed the right people in the right places.

They would scrutinize them and correct any faults from them and solve any grievances they caused to the people. They appointed knowledgeable, honest and wise people as their representatives and Governors in the ever increasing areas and territories which included all the Arabian Peninsulas Syria and Iraq in the north, Persia and beyond in the east, and Egypt in the West! in their time all these areas became under the Islamic rule.

These successors of Prophet *Mohammad* were known as and are called the Khalifa (Caliph) Rashedeen or the pious successors of the Prophet and they were:

1. **Abu-bakr Al Siddiq**   2. **Omer ibn Al Khattab**
3. **Othman ibn Affan**   4. **Ali ibn Abu Taleb**

ABU BAKR AL SIDDIQ THE FIRST CALIPH OR SUCCESSOR.

He was the first Caliph of Islam after the death of Prophet *Mohammad* (Peace be upon him). When the Prophet died many people in Madinah were in shock, and did not believe the news of his death. Among them was Omer who later on became the second Caliph. Omer was so shocked with the news of the death of the Prophet that he swore to kill any one who would say that prophet *Mohammad* (peace be upon him) is dead. He thought that *Mohammad* would never die, and that he may have been elevated or raised to heaven, but not dead.

But Abu Bakr did nothing of these. He accepted the news calmly and went straight to the house of the Prophet. He saw his child-hood friend, *Mohammad* (peace be upon him), lying on his deathbed. He kissed his forehead and his cheeks and said calmly "I adore you more than my father and my Mother O Prophet of Allah, and you look as good when you are dead as when you were alive. And then he read the verse from the Qur'an. "We all belong to Allah and to Him we return."

Then he came out of the Prophets house and entered the Mosque (The Prophets house was connected or adjacent to the Mosque). He climbed the steps of the stand or pulpit and called for the attention of the people who gathered there after hearing the news. The people in the mosque were all eyes and ears towards Abu Bakr. He gave a small speech; wherein he thanked Allah and praised Him and said the blessings and peace on the Prophet, and then said "for those people who would worship *Mohammad*, *Mohammad* is dead. And for those who worship Allah, Allah is ever alive and will never die." Then he read verses from the Qur'an Thus:

"Mohammad is but a messenger, messengers (the like of whom) have passed away before him. Will it be that, when he dieth or is slain, ye will turn back on your heels? He who turneth back do not hurt to Allah, and Allah will reward the thankful." { Al Imran:144}

After hearing these verses of the Qur'an from Abu Bakr, most of the people were calmed down and came to their senses, as they fully became aware of its meanings Every one in this world will die, regardless of who it would be.

Abu Bakr was the child-hood friend of *Mohammad* in Makkah. He knew his friend *Mohammad* (peace be upon him) never said a lie, and when he informed him about the revelation of Qur'an and the order to propagate Islam Abu Bakr was the first among his friends who believed in him and accepted Islam immediately and without hesitance. He started propagating Islam himself. And among those who became Muslims through him in the beginning of Islam was his friend Othman, the third Caliph of Islam. During the migration of the Prophet from Makkah to Madinah, Abu Bakr was his companion and stayed with him in the cave for three days before they proceeded to Madinah.

Abu Bakr also became among the relatives of the Prophet as he gave his daughter Aysha in marriage to Prophet *Mohammad* (peace be upon him), when they were in Madinah.

The second day after the Prophet died Abu Bakr was elected the 1st Caliph or successor of the Prophet, and became the first leader of Islam after Prophet *Mohamma*d (peace be upon him), after the leaders of the Muhajreen and Ansar in Madinah held council, and elected him for this position. That was the first election in Islam, and so were his successors who also were elected as such.

Abu Bakr was Caliph for a short period of about two years and seven months when he died, after establishing and solidifying the authority of Islam in the Arabian Peninsula. Especially when he crushed the rebellion in the eastern part of the peninsula which flared up immediately after the prophet died. They refused to accept the third principle of Islam and pay the Zakat. This situation could not be allowed, otherwise the other principles would disintegrate in no time, and consequently other Islamic principles will disintegrate.

In the time of Abu Bakr's caliphate period the Qur'an was gathered, collected and arranged as it was originally used to be read at the time of the Prophet *Mohammad* (peace be upon him)and his followers.

AMEER AL MOMINEEN OMER IBN AL KHATTAB THE SECOND CALIPH:

In the beginning Omer was among the fiercest enemies of *Mohammad* and Islam. He was big tall and was feared by all who knew him. One day he put his sword on his belt and left his house on the way to kill *Mohammad* (peace be upon him). On the way he was stopped by a friend who asked him "where are you going and why you look so furious." Omer replied that he was on his way going to kill *Mohammad* and get rid of him and his propagation, once and for all.

His friend said why do you want to kill him, did you not know that your own sister and brother in law also became Muslims. Why don't you become like them. This thing shook him. He changed his course and went instead to his sister's house. When his sister knew of his arrival at the door, she and her husband hid the papers where in verses of the Qur'an were written, and which they were reading at that time. Omer entered their house, and the first thing he asked was: "what were you reading" because he had heard them reciting when he came. At first his sister denied that she was reading anything, which made him angry and he slapped her face. Instead of becoming afraid or scared, she became furious and shouted at him "yes we were reading verses from the Qur'an, and we became Muslims." He was stunned, because his sister never challenged him or shouted back at him before.

Then he asked to see the paper - she told him he cannot touch that holy paper until he washes and cleans himself. He did that, and then she read for him some of the verses of the Qur'an. (Surat TAHA) He was amazed - Because he never heard such a sentences or verses before. He knew that this is not a saying of human beings and it is not poetry. He then realized that this was the truth he heard. And so his mind and character changed.

He told his sister and her husband that he left home with the intention to kill *Mohammad* before he came to them. And now he is going to seek *Mohammad* because he wants to become a Muslim and embrace Islam. So he went to see *Mohammad* (peace be upon him) in his hiding place, a small house in Makkah and announced his intention to become a Muslim. Prophet *Mohammad* (peace be upon him) was delighted by this turn of events. Because Omer gave a big boost to the small number of scared followers of *Mohammad* (peace be upon him) and his religion Islam. Omar was the answer of the prayer of the Prophet when he prayed Allah to show the light and benefit Islam by either of the two Omar's. (Omar ibn Al Khattab or Omro bin Hisham, who was known as Abo Jahl.)

From this hiding place Omer went straight to the "Lion's den" He went to where all the Quraish leaders and their followers usually assemble and gather to discuss their affairs or worship their idols around the Ka'abah. When he reached there he announced openly that he became Muslim and he would dare anyone who would challenge him. People used to fear Omer, but this time he challenged them right at their idols place, and they were so many in number. So a fight erupted where he beat many of them but he was also beaten very well, as he was out numbered.

After Omer joined the group of Muslims and became part of them he became a close friend and companion of the Prophet. The followers of *Mohamma*d (peace be upon him) began rising in number and started coming out openly to announce their new religion.

After the death of Abu Bakr the 1st Caliph, Omer was chosen to be the second Caliph of Islam. He was the leader of the Muslim world for the next thirteen years - which were the Golden era of Islam and the Muslims. In his period Islam expanded to far away places. Also the city of Jerusalem was given to him without a fight, because he was known for his justice and order.

Omer was a strict observer of the religious duties and also strict enforcer of the law. He lived a life of poverty and many a time the visiting emissaries, ambassadors and dignitaries were astounded to see him dressed in his old and tattered clothes. Many a time when they visited Madinah to meet him they were surprised to find him lying under a tree near the Prophet's mosque, when they were expecting to meet this great leader in a palace fit for kings.

At night he make rounds in the streets of Madinah. He would help the poor and sick people and the widows and the old people and orphans. He became known as the guardian of all the needy, wretched and poor people. And in the daytime he attended to his court in the Prophets Mosque and did the state affairs.

Justice among the people was among the main concerns of this great leader. In his time, the son of the viceroy or governor of Egypt Amer ibn Al Aas hit his competitor, a commoner, when he won a horseracing contest between them. He hit the boy because he ignored his position as the son of the Governor and still tried and won the race against him.

The father of the grieved son took his son and came to Madinah to meet the Caliph and put his grievance to him. Omer the Caliph summoned his Governor from Egypt to come immediately and to bring his son with him. When they came to Madinah and the Caliph found the claim of the Egyptian to be true he gave the son of the Egyptian the whip and ordered him to hit the son of the Governor as hard as he was hit by him, in front of all the people in court. And then he said his famous saying "since when did you enslave people while their mothers gave birth to them as free persons." He believes that justice delayed is equal to injustice in the life of the people. And he didn't differentiate between a mighty Government employee and a normal citizen, or between a rich and a poor one.

In his time Islam reached far away places. And he appointed known pious and good character persons as his emissaries and Governors in all the places. And he used to take account of their work from time to time. No corruption in government affair was allowed. He was a great leader, and was firm but fair with his generous and emissaries he appointed through out the large Islamic state.

In his time the Islamic state expanded Syria to Iraq, Persia and the north eastern part of Asia in the east and Egypt and some parts of North Africa in the east.

After fabulous era of peace and justice one day he was stabled in his back by a non-believer while leading the morning prayers in the mosque in Madinah. He died three days later.

His was the most glorious and fabulous era for Islam where justice and wealth was abounds and it was the most stable Islamic state in his time.

AMEER AL MOMINEEN (PRINCE OF THE BELIEVERS):

Omer was the successor of Abu Bakr the first Caliph who was the successor of the Prophet. Thus his title was (Caliph, Caliphate Rasool Allah) (The successor of the Prophet's successor) a long title !

One day some emissaries from his Governor in Kofa or Iraq came to Madianh on an official errand. They asked about Omer the Caliph: "Where is Ameer Al Momineen"?! or where is the prince of the believers. His companions liked this short and new title for the Caliph so they suggested to the caliph Omer to use it, and he accepted it. And from that time this title was used, and the Caliphs or successors after him used it. And since then it became the official or formal title of Muslim rulers and was used by the succeeding caliphs of the Prophet.

One day while he was offering prayers and leading the morning congregation he was stabbed by a non believer. He died three days later, and was buried beside his two dear friends Prophet *Mohammad* (peace be upon him) and Abu Bakr the first Caliph. Omer was among the great leaders in Islam. In his time Islamic state was solidified and expanded beyond the Arabian peninsula into Egypt in Africa and all through Iraq and Persia in Asia and all the northern parts of the Arabian peninsula .

AMEER AL MOMINEEN OTHMAN IBN AFFAN THE 3RD CALIPH:

He was born in Makkah in the 6th year after the Elephant invasion of Makkah, or 576 (AD) He was from a noble and rich family. And he was Abu Bakr's friend. When Abu Bakr become Muslim he invited Othman to do so, to which he readily agreed and he became a Muslim.

He was related to the Prophet from his mother's side as she was the daughter of his Aunt Al Baida'a, Um Hakim. He was a very handsome gentleman, and used to dress well, as he came from a rich and noble family of Makkah.

He married two daughters of the Prophet. First he was married to Ruqaya, and he migrated with her to Ethiopia with the first batch of immigrants who went there. After a while he returned back to Makkah, and when the migration to Madinah was opened, he too migrated to Madinah.

He accompanied the Prophet on all his missions and incursions, except the incursion of Badr. He could not go on this incursion because his wife Roqaya was sick, and the Prophet gave him permission to stay back to look after her. Mean while she died. When the war in Badr ended, and the Prophet returned back to Madinah, he gave his second daughter Umm-Kulthum in marriage to Othman. Thus he became known as Zu-Al Noorain - indicating him as the holder of the two lights from the house of the Prophet.

He was gentle, pious and very knowledgeable in Islamic teachings and remembered all of the holy Qur'an by heart. He was a natural calligraphist and had scribed and written the Qur'an with his own writing- by hand. He was generous. He bought handsomely from his own sources, the Rumma Well and dug it wider, as it was the main source of water in Madinah, and let it be used freely by the residents of Madinah. They used to pay costly to buy the water from its previous owners. This he did when the Prophet asked who would alleviate the hardship of the people by buying this well and allocate its use to the people. So he voluntarily did this noble job, in the name of Allah - without asking compensation for it.

In another occasion he furnished and fully equipped hundreds of mules and horses for the Islamic army on one of its incursions on his own, without charging any cost to them. This also is among his noble charities he did on the suggestion of the Prophet, and in the name of Allah. He also bought the piece of land next to the Prophet Mosque and annexed it and expanded the Prophets Mosques for the ever increasing numbers of Muslims who would come for congregation in it.

Ameer Al Momineen Othman was chosen from six of the Prophet's close companions three days after the assassination of the second Caliph Omer. He accepted the job of the Caliph and became the third Caliph of Islam.

He was lenient in his rule as against Omer who was strong in character. He used to listen to the people and used to change his governors and emissaries on their complaints. This agitated many of his emissaries. Specially the ones in Koufa, Basra and Egypt, who later on made a conspiracy against him.

They sent some of their bandits or terrorists to Madinah, who climbed on the house he was living in, and assassinated him while he was reading the holy Qur'an. He was Caliph for about 12 years. His time as caliph was among the longest.

He was known for his fine handwriting and as a calligraphist he wrote the Holy Qur'an by his own hand.

AMEER AL MOMINEEN ALI BIN ABU TALEB THE FOURTH CALIPH

Ali was the cousin of the Prophet. As a child he was taken care of by the Prophet and was brought up in his household. In recognition of his uncle's kindness to him while he was a child, and to take off some of the burden from his uncle Abu Taleb, *Mohammad* Prophet *Mohammad* (peace be upon him) took care of Ali when he was young.

Ali was the first to accept Islam among the children. He grew up in the Prophet's house, and was married to the Propeht's daughter Fatima. When the Prophet decided to leave Makkah and migrate to Madinah - Ali was there to help him. The Prophet entrusted him with all the deposits and consignments he had in trust with him, so that he would give back those belongings to its owners. The Prophet also asked Ali to sleep in his own bed as camouflage - the night he left for Madinah. Few days after the Prophet's arrival in Madinah, Ali also arrived with his wife Fatima, the youngest daughter of the Prophet, after complying with the Prophet's orders - and paid back all the trusts to their owners, before coming to Madinah.

Ali was the cousin of the Prophet, he married his daughter Fatima, and their sons Al Hasan and Al Husein were the Prophet's grand children, who grew up in his house and the Prophet used to love them very much. Ali and his sons are known as the Prophets family (Aal Al Bait).

Ali became the fourth Caliph after caliph Othman's death. He was the Caliph for three years. The turmoil which began at the time of Othman continued also in the time of Ali, and eventually he was also assassinated by one of those killers who conspired to kill Ali, Moawiyah and Amr ibn Al Aas. He was killed while he was out of his house in Koufa - calling the believers for the Fajr (Morning) prayer, and was assassinated during his prayer.

These are the four Caliphs or successors of the Prophet. They uphold the teachings of Islam, and during their time and rule the Islamic state became well established, solidified and expended to far out places east and west.

They were the most pious and righteous successors of the Prophet and who were personally disinterested in the worldly affairs and pomps.

After these Caliphs Rashideen, things changed as Moawiyah bin Abu Sufyan became the ruler and he made his son the viceroy and appointed him his successor, there by opening the way for monarchy among the Islamic states.

THE FOUR SCHOOLS OR SCHOLARS OF THOUGHTS IN ISLAM:

The Caliph's of the Prophet (his successors) were the rulers, political leaders and themselves were highly trained scholars of Islam. And in their time there were many companions of the Prophet among the people they were leading.

But in later generations there were some learned scholars who taught the people in their time and era all the teachings of Islam and explained those teachings by words and their own deeds, as the leaders or rulers of their era were themselves in need of knowledge of the Islamic teachings. Hence there were those learned scholars who helped in educating the people and had created their own way which were derived from their understanding of various matters of religion and they taught people those standards.

Among the many learned scholars there were four well known and famous scholars who one after the other helped in promoting their knowledge, thoughts or discipline. These schools of thought are from the teachings of the four well-known scholars of Islam, and Emams of their time.

They were:

1. **Emam Abu Hanifah** **(150 AH) 767 AD) – Hanafi.**

2. **Emam Malik ibn Anas** **(93 – 179 AH – Maliki.**

3. **Emam *Mohammad* bin Idrees Al Shafie (150-204 AH) – Shafie.**

4. **Emam Ahmad bin Hanbal (164-241 AH) – Hanbali.**

Those schools are named after the scholars or founders of those schools of thoughts. The four scholars who preceded each other in different times had their different ways which they each knew, understood and interpret, what the deeds and actions and sayings of the Prophet they understood, or how they understood it, differently. And they all obtained their knowledge from the same fountain or source it came from. That source as a necessity comes from the Qur'an and the sunnah which are the sayings, deeds and actions of the prophet of Islam *Mohammad* (Peace be upon him). The difference of their teachings comes from their own way of understanding what they thought or believed it to be the most right way, to observe and perform some of the rituals and obligations, and in the understandings of the procedure as they saw it to be the most proper. And people in their era or generation followed their understanding as they were the most famous or popular scholars in their time.

Fundamentally, they all are the same in their central theme and the belief, or crux of the matter. The difference mostly comes in the way to understand and apply it. And as such all the four schools make and complete each other's thinking.. They do not differ in any basic belief or understanding of Islam. Their difference is in the application of slight variations in the performance of some of the rituals and adhering to it as they saw or understand. And so do their followers who would follow those scholars in their teachings.

CHAPTER 12

THE SOURCES AND CONTINUITY OF ISLAM

THE SOURCE OF ISLAM:

After learning what we did so far about Islam and its teachings and its messages to humanity, we would like to know the source of continuity of all the knowledge and teachings Muslims receives, understands, obeys and adheres to these messages and teachings.

These are the two main sources:

1.   **The Holy Qur'an**

2.   **The Prophet *Mohammad* – his sayings and deeds.**

3.   **To follow the foot-steps of the companions**

One is the divine book which is the constitution of this religion, and the other is the verbal and practical explanations with his sayings & deeds. The third is to follow the footstep of the companions who have recieved their teachings from the prophet, and the scholars thereafter.

THE HOLY QUR'AN:

This is the holy and divine book from where Muslims get their knowledge and blessings of Allah. The holy book The Qur'an is the constitutional or policy book for Muslims. They will adhere to whatever rules and regulations there into it. It provides them with solace and inner comfort when they read it .

It gives an inner peace and tranquility to the believers.

The Qur'an began with the first revelations which was revealed upon Prophet *Mohammad* (peace be upon him) in the cave of Heraá and with its revelations began the era of propagation of Islam.

In his youth, *Mohammad* (Peace be upon him) used to go to a cave in Hira'a mountain. Unlike other youths who may spend their time in vain, he used to go there and meditate and think for long hours. Until one day the Arch Angel Gabriel came to him. *Mohammad* was startled by the sudden presence of some one whom he did not know or expect.

The Angel asked *Mohammad* to read. He did not know what to read. He did not even know how to read. So he said, "I am not a reader". The Angel then embraced *Mohammad* with force until his body was aching. And then released him and again told him to read. To which *Mohammad* again replied, "I am not a reader" meaning he did not know what to read, He was again embraced by Angel Gabriel until he was perspiring, and then released him. Then he told *Mohammad* to (recite after him),

In the name of your Lord who created (all that exists)* He has created man from a clot* Recite, and your Lord is the most Generous, who has taught (the writing) by pen, He has taught human that He did not know. (Surah Al-alaq)

And *Mohammad* recited after him, this was the first time the Qur'anic verses were revealed unto *Mohammad*, and this is where and when the revelations started to be bestowed upon him, and made him the Prophet and Messenger of Allah to all the people of the world to preach and propagate the teachings of Islam.

God says about *Mohammad* in the Qur'an (**And we did not send you except as merciful for all the worlds.**)

From this date which is about 13 years before the Prophet migrated to Madinah, and 10 years there-after. Until shortly before his death these revelations continued to come in. It came in stages and whenever situation required during the 23 years of its revelations unto the Prophet.

At the time of the Prophet, he and most of his companions preserved and learned by heart, whatever was revealed of the Qur'an. Some of them were good writers, and they would write whatever revealed to the Prophet as he dictates it to them immediately after its revelations unto him. They would write on whatever material available at that time that they could use. The Prophet would ask the ones who wrote the verses to read and recite back to him to find if it was correctly written or recorded according to how the Prophet received and recited it for them. And whenever a new revelation would come he would recite it with the Angel Gabriel and then the Prophet advises his companions and writers to put it in its proper place as indicated to him by the Angel. All these manuscripts were kept safely in the Prophets house and in the order it have been revealed unto the Prophet.

During the last month of Ramadan before the Prophet died, the Arch angel Gabriel came twice, and in both times the Prophet would recite all the Qur'an with him to make sure that he memorized it exactly as it was revealed unto him, and all verses or sentences are in its proper place. And some of his companions would write and recite it as they would hear it from the Prophet (peace be upon him). It was in written form as scriptures when the Prophet died, and there were several companions who would memorize and scribe copies for themselves. But the main documents were kept with the Prophet in his house.

Few years after the Prophet's death, in one of the battles a big number of the Prophets companions who had learned and memorized the Qur'an by heart died. This situation brought a great deal of concern to the Prophet's companions, and upon the advice of Omer, Caliph Abu Bakr appointed Zaid bin Thabet, to collect the transcript and put it in a book form. (Zaid bin Thabet was one of the trusted companions of the Prophet, and whom the Prophet would delegate the task of scribing the verses for him along with other of his companions, whenever it was revealed). Beside scribing or writing, these companions would also memorize and read it to the Prophet, and he used to direct them where to place each and every verse, and they were able to do this job properly. So Abu Bakr appointed Zaid and gave him the task to write and make one official volume of the holy Qur'an. Zaid along with other trustworthy companions and colleagues collected the manuscripts from many people who used to and did write these revelations when it was revealed on Prophet *Mohammad* (peace be upon him), and started to compile it in accordance with the Prophets original instructions. This was not a closed door task, but it was an open door public affair where all the Prophet's companions would be able to help. (Excerpts from the book "Index of Qur'anic topics")

This first official volume of the Qur'an prepared under the supervision of Zaid was put under the custody of Abu Bakr - and from him it was passed over to the second Caliph Omer, who in turn kept it with his daughter Hafsa, a widow of the Prophet.

During the time of the 3rd. Caliph Othman ibn Affan many people who newly joined Islam and whose main language was not Arabic were reading the Qur'an in different modes and dialects. When told about this, Caliph Othman asked Zaid and his team to scribe and make copies of the first volume of the Qur'an they have made at the time of the 1st Caliph Abu Bakr, and made several copies of it. And those copies were sent over to all the different parts of the Islamic state as an official copy - to avoid all future confusions. And as the Qur'an's authenticity have been assured by Allah who thus mentions:

"It is We who have sent down the Qur'an; and We will preserve it."

Qur'an is always preserved from corruptions. This is vouched and promised by Allah.

WHAT IS IN THE QUR'AN?

Among the divine scriptures, Quràn is the last and final book which was revealed in parts and parcels during the period of about 23 years of the mission of Prophet *Mohammad* (peace be upon him). It is one of the most important and significant miracles, bestowed unto him. Qur'an reveals to all mankind the beginning or the history of the universe and the things in it. It is mentioned in the form of revelations for us to understand and observe the meanings and lessons humans can derive from the revelations in it.

It is a book for all times. It tells what inspired and happened in the past, it shows what is happening now and it reveals what is going to happen or occur in the future. In it we can see what is happening during our lifetime and what may be expected in the life after death. It gives us hope as human beings, if we do the things we were told to do, (all the good things in life), and it warns us of what could be expected as punishment in our lifetime, and the life after death, if we do not abstain or refrain from doing bad or evil things or deeds which we were told not to do. (all the wrong doings).

It tells us about heaven, wherein good people who did good deeds and said good things during their lifetime, and believed in God and in His oneness are expected to be going to. It clearly shows us what will happen in hell to those who did bad and evil things, and did not believe in God and in His Oneness. Qur'an shows the way to do lots of good things in life to deserve the blessings and happiness in this life, and live in Heaven and enjoy its fabulous life thereafter. It also clearly tells us why and how to abstain from doing bad deeds during our life time, so that we can avoid being punished and thrown in hell, later on.

It mentions and encompasses all that exists in His creations, and without which we as humans could not understand and comprehend. It describes the celestial revolutions and its path in the universe and how exact is the movement of all those stars, planets and the sun and the moon. There is no deviations in the movements of any of these, except for the normal variations designed meticulously. And it would mean its destruction, if it deviates from its path or its revolutions, and all things connected in its path. For instance if the earth were slightly closer to the sun from where it is now, everything in it would be a towering inferno, or if the earth were slightly away or farther from where it is supposed to be from the sun, then all and everything in it would be freezing to death. This is all said and explained so well that it will make us believe whole heartedly in God and His power of doing whatever He wishes.

Suppose the gravity or gravitation of the earth is increased slightly, do you think anything on it could move on with the same ease and precision it is doing now. Can we make airplane or rockets which can leave this planet and fly for few miles?! Also, if the gravity is lighter than what it is now, can any normal life be expected on earth or everything would be floating around - aimlessly. These things have to be considered by humans as God has described thus in His first revelations to the Prophet:

He taught man that what he knew not. (or whatever way) verily, man does transgress (in disbelief and evil deed.)

Because he considers himself, self sufficient (man thinks he knows everything) (Surat Al Alaq 5,6,7)

There is this revelation about the sun and the moon and how day and night evolve:

And the sun runs on its fixed course for a term (appointed) that is the decree of the Almighty, who knows all. And the moon, we have measured for its mansions (traverse) till it returns like the old dried curved stalk of date.

It is not for the sun to overtake the moon, nor does the night outstrip the day. They all float, each in (its) orbit. (Yasin 38,39,40)

And in other revelations in the Qur'an:

It was He who gave the sun its brightness and the Moon its light, ordaining its phases that you may learn to count the years (compute the seasons) God created them only to manifest the truth. He makes plain His revelations to men who understand. In the alternation of night and day, and in all that God has created in the heavens and earth, there are signs for righteous men, (yonus 4-5)

In the Qur'an there are in many places revelations of the creation of human, in such a detailed form that only books of physics or of medicine would reveal such detailed way of the creations of humans today. After the creation of ADAM from clay and EVE there-after, comes the development and creation of humans, that modern science and medicine did understand and confirm it now. It explains this creation from when it is conceived from a drop of sperm, and the stages or phases going through from sperm to be a clot hanging and becoming an embryo and the slow development of his whole body in his mothers' womb, where his limbs and bone are created and then how are the bones covered with flesh, until he is born. This is a miraculous revelation which was revealed about 1424 years ago. When this human is created from such a small drop of sperm, he becomes a man with strong body and instead of thanking God for his creation he starts arguing with Him, His creator the God Almighty, and may not even believe in Him. Beside the detailed description of the creation of human beings in many different places and parts of this Holy book, God also tells us that He made the humans of thinking, gave them the mind. And through this mind human was made capable of differentiating between the good and the bad, the right and the wrong. Allah also tells us that he himself created man in the best from and feature and made him the best and the noblest of all his creatures.

This divine scripture and holy book contains among its abilities the healing capability. It may be spiritual, psychological or physical ailments. By reading in this book the believers find solace and comfort and hope in their life.:

"It is guidance and healing for those who believe". (Fussilat - 44)

It is a light which shines our way, and gives us solace and comfort spiritually as well as mentally. The Quràn was revealed unto Prophet *Mohammad* (peace be upon him) in Arabic language, which was his mother tongue, and it was sent and meant for all the humanity. The language it was revealed in is the most superb and versatile form of Arabic that no human could or can produce or compose such a high level of verses and sentences, even from among the most learned people, past or present.

This holy book is preserved in its original form (as Allah Himself promised to preserve it), since it was revealed about 1425 years ago. The whole book has been learnt by memory and remembered by heart, by millions of people today, as it has been on-going since the prophet's time. This is part of the miracles that this book itself is. It gives an inner peace and tranquility and solace to the believers who read it. The Qur'an gives much blessing when it is read, deliberated upon and implemented. The mere recitation of the Quar'an is a blessing.

Any verses from the Qur'an mentioned in this book I tried to obtain its translations, from various versions of translations to be as near to its likely meaning in the Qur'an as much as possible.

2. The other most important source of Islamic teachings we receive is from Prophet *Mohammad* (peace be upon him): His sayings and deeds.

Upon whom the Qur'an was revealed and whose sayings and deeds becomes the main source of belief in Islam. During his lifetime and before he was proclaimed as the Messenger and Prophet of Allah, *Mohammad* was an exemplary person in his sayings and deeds. And the Quraan Vouches for the authenticity of his saying, thus:

By the star when it fells down. Your companion is not astray nor misled. And he does not utter a thing of

his desire. But it is inspiration that is revealed unto him. He was taught by the Powerful Almighty. (53 : 2-3-4)

Muslims follows his footstep in their life activities. Especially in the most important form of their life which is the prayers and worshiping of Allah and all other religious functions and rituals, which he verbally and practically shown and explained.

In his youth *Mohammad* was known and famous for being righteousness and was called "Al Ameem" or the righteous or the trust worthy person, because he always spoks the truth. Muslims follow his teachings by what he says which they obey, and by his deeds which they follow.

During his lifetime and after his death most of the sayings of the prophet were remembered and collected by his companions and followers. His companions used to observes his doings and try to follow them as much as they can. They remember his sayings and follow it to the letter.

THE HADITH OF THE PROPHET

In the beginning of the third century (AH), few famous scholars like Al Bukhari and Muslim, came to collect and write whatever they could get of the sayings and doings of the prophet. They would ask people of any Hadith (or Sayings) of the Prophet they knew or heard it from their ancestors or forefathers, and who knew or heard it from the companions of the prophet who saw him or heard from him, in their lifetime, to make it in a book form for future generation's to read and follow.

They would write and register as much of the sayings, and deeds of the Prophet and from several sources, that they would follow and ask. This way they authenticated most of what they have written down, of the activities, doings and sayings of the Prophet. And when they were satisfied with the authenticity of those Hadith's, they would record it with the names of those different people or sources who gave them these information's, and the way it reached to them. There are other Scholars who attempted and gathered similar information, which added to enrich the Islamic heritage. These collections are called the "Hadith" or the sayings of the Prophet, and it is referred to in case of any doubt of what we should follow from these sayings and activities. Since we knew that the holy book The Qur'an is the constitution and policy book, we should also know that the Hadith or the sayings and deeds of the Prophet are the practical explanation, clarification and working manual of this holy book.

(And when I refer to these sayings in this book I write, "and which means", where in we try to avoid any error we may unintentionally incur in the translations of the Hadith. Sometime it is difficult to put the exact wordings or interpretations of these sayings).

(3) To follow the foot-steps of the companions of the Prophet

There are other sources strictly derived from the two main sources of teachings of Islam. These are:

(a)   To follow the sayings and deeds of the Prophets Companions who were with him most of the time, and they used to observe and follow his footsteps. They taught their own children and family members of the way they learned from the sayings and deeds of the Prophet (peace be upon him), when they were with him, and they themselves saw him and listened to him personally.

(b)   And there are the scholars of Islam who did their utmost to find truth and explain things which are difficult to understand and put it in their books and studies. They tried to translate, interpret and explain the meanings of the verses or sentences of the Quràn, and the reason behind the revelations of those verses and sentences and the time it was revealed and the occasion for that. They tried to adhere themselves to what they could find from earlier generations, and explain it to the later generations. They are the industrious and hard working diligent scholars. There are many well learned Scholars who took time to write and explain what ordinary people may not have understood. So we follow their books which describes and interpret what was revealed in the Qur'an and also how the Prophet followed and explained what came in it.

THE HEALING ABILITY OF HONEY IN THE QUR'AN:

As mentioned earlier the Qur'an carries many miracles and encompass all aspects of human life. This is a short description about the honey which is mentioned in the Qur'an. Before that, I would like to mention a personal experience. Many years ago I took my children on a short vacation. There in the hotels swimming pool, my young son without realizing, dived in shallow water. Seeing the mistake he made he tried to pull himself from hitting the bottom of the pool.

Even with this instant maneuver he did receive a bruise on his cheek and a deep cut on his eye brow. When he came out of the pool his face was covered with blood dripping from the cut he received on his eye brow. Hotel doctor came and after examining the cut advised that he should be taken to hospital as he needed few stitches, which made the child and his young sisters scared.

So to calm them down I took them to the room and asked him to take a shower. In the meantime I asked for some honey which luckily every hotel's have. After coming out of shower and dried down I put little honey on the wound and closed it with a band-aid.

This instinct medical aid I learned from the Holy Qur'an where in it is mentioned about the honey that it have healing capability for people (human beings).:

Your Lord inspired the bee, saying: 'Make your homes in the mountains, in the trees, and in the hives which men shall build for you. Then Feed on every kind of fruit, and follow the trodden paths of your Lord.' From its belly comes forth a syrup of different hues, where in a healing (a cure) for mankind. Surely in this there is a sign for those who would give thought. (Al-Nahl 16:68,69)

After the next day my son asked if he can go to swim I told him that he cannot swim until his wound is healed - To which he smilingly removed the band-aid and showed me only a trace of thin line where the wound was. The wound was healed. This is a personal experience I liked to share with the readers.

At the time of the Prophet a worried man told the prophet that his brother was suffering a pain in his stomach. The Prophet advised to give him some honey. Eventually after two/three days of using honey his brother was healed.

Scientist now are taking keen interest in this subject, and in a recent study it was found that honey contains a strong Antibiotic medicine which can destroy the super Bug bacteria known as MRSA (Methicillin Resistant Staphylococcus Aureus.) which no other medicine could do so easily.

The healing capability of Honey mentioned in the Qur'an without specifics or limitations of the ailments which it can cure. And as such its healing power for known or unknown ailments will be boundless, besides being nourishing and invigorating food.

CHAPTER
13

THE MOSQUE

THE MOSQUES:

In Muslim/Islamic countries we see thousands of people entering hundreds of mosques in each and every city, five times a day. It is more so on Friday's. They enter these mosques to offer their prayers. Mosques are known as houses of Allah. Primarily a mosque is built to worship in it. It is a gathering place where the people in the surrounding area can come and do their prayers in congregation.

"The Mosques are (built for Allah so invoke no one at all) along with Allah." { 72:18}

Islam emphasizes on its followers to attend the Mosques and encourages them to pray and worship Allah in it, together in congregation five times a day.

Besides being a religious gathering place it also becomes a place for social activities where the social affairs of the believers may be discussed and the grievances are rectified. Here the Emam may give sermon or speech and sheds light on the affairs of Muslims. In mosques people come to know each other because of their religious routine, which is the obligatory five time prayers each and every day. No days-off, or weekend from prayers. This way people in the community will know each other and may come closer. They will get to know each other, the children become friendly with each other. The women who attend their prayers in Mosques also get to know each other. This way people in each area around the Mosques become friendly and socialize, instead of being aloof or strangers towards each other. They may say hello - how are you, shyly in the beginning, but then they may become good friends in the long run.

After his migration Prophet *Mohammad* (peace be upon him) arrived in a place called Quba'a, in Madinah. He stayed there for a brief period; and while he was there he built the first Mosques in Islam The Quba Mosque.. That Mosque is still there in Medinah, since 1425 years, and it has been renovated many times since then. It was renovated and expanded during the time of King Fahd of Saudi Arabia recently.

Later on the Prophet moved to proper Madinah in the center of the town. He obtained a peace of land, and on it built his house and beside his house he built the Mosque. This is known as the Prophets Mosques and it is regarded as the second most holy Mosque in Islam after the Al Haram Mosque in Makkah which contains the Kaabah. The third most holy Mosque is the Al Aqsa Mosque in Jerusalem, Palestine. Islam emphasizes on the building of Mosques and regards it among the most charitable acts by its followers. Even though it is permissible to offer the prayers in any clean and neat place, and at home or in the work places, it stresses more on the Muslims to attend the Mosques for their obligatory payers and worships, in congregation. Especially the Friday prayers where they listen to the sermon given by the Emam, before offering the congregational two Raka'at prayers.

The Mosques are recognized by two significant symbols the Dome and the Minarets (or towers). The Dome gives an impressive view from outside and also inside the Mosques. The minarets are used as towers, where in climbs the Maouzine or a caller to give a call for prayers in the proper timings.

Like all the Islamic constructions the minarets were also developed from short tower on the roof, where the Maouzine would climb and call for prayers for every one to hear, until it became big and taller during the years to come, and in the big cities. With the time the minarets and the dome became the symbol or significant marks of the Mosques. Now with the present advanced audio systems around the world, these minarets are but a symbol of the past when there was not even a loudspeaker available. The other most important part inside the Mosques is the (Menber) the dais or pulpit on which the Emem (the one who leads the congregation in prayers) or the Khateeb of the Jumaa or Friday prayers will stand and deliver speech or sermon every Friday, or whenever occasion require.

THE THREE HOLY MOSQUES IN MAKKAH, MADINAH AND JERUSALEM:

Building Mosques is a highly rewarded work of charity, and it is urged and encouraged in Islam. To visit and worship in the mosques is an important obligations, on Muslims. God said in the Qur'an which means:

"The Mosques of Allah shall be built (visited and maintained) by those who believe in Allah and the last day (day of Judgment), and performed (his) prayers, and paid the Zakat (Tax for the Poor) and feared none but Allah, It is they who are on true guidance." { 9:18}

All mosques built everywhere are important and holy places. But there are the three most significant and most holy mosques which are:

Al Masjid Al Haram (Holy Mosque) in Makkah
Masjid Al Rasool (Prophet's Mosque) in Madianh
Masjid Al Aqsa (Aqsa Mosque) in Jersulaem.

THE HOLY MOSQUE IN MAKKAH:

This is the most sacred and holy place for Muslims in the world. Because it is built around the House of God, the Holy Kaabah. After the conquest of Makkah in the 8th year (AH) (after the migration) (630AD). Muslims performed prayers in rows around the Kaabah. It was an open place, then.

During the era of the second Caliph of Islam Omer ibn Al Khatab a huge flood destroyed some parts of the Kaabah. He visited Makkah and ordered its repair and also built a short wall or fence around it. So that people can pray and worship inside this fence, after he obtained the land and bought the properties houses surrounding the Kaabah. As the number of believers who were coming to Makkah to perform Hajj and Omra was ever increasing, the need to expand the Mosque became necessary. The second Caliph Omer did again expanded the area which was built earlier. After Omer came the third Caliph Otheman ibn Affan who also bought more lands and properties to expand this Mosque and built it bigger. And since that time this Grand Mosque became bigger and bigger until it became one of the biggest worshipping place of its time, today. - besides being the holiest for all Muslims.

Many of the Caliphs and rulers of Islam have endeavored in the building, renovation and expansion of this mosque throughout history. Among the great expansions and modern builders are the Othman rulers of Turkey, who did a great job after the big expansion at the time of the Abbasid ruler Al Mahdi.

The latest and the biggest and most modern expansion is at present time which was carried out in the Saudi era, starting with King Abdulaziz Al Saud, and that of the custodian of the two holy Mosques King Fahad. Most modern equipment and technical expertise was employed to build this Grand Mosque in the Islamic architecture. It has the most modern system of ventilation, refrigeration and air-conditioning to help cool down the atmosphere in this open building. Special white marble which does not absorb heat, was used on the floor in the tawaf area. Now even during the hot summer days and at noontime, worshippers can walk around the Kaabah bare footed, and would not feel the heat, which used to burn their feet, in the old days. At present this mosque may carry about 2 million worshippers. This includes the ground level, the second floor and the rooftop of this mosque, besides the open area surrounding it. This is a miraculous job done and completed in the year 1415 AH (1995 AD). It will be one of the greatest monuments in history, besides its sanctity as the holiest Mosques in Islam.

Prophet *Mohammad* (peace be upon him) says in one of his hadith or sayings which means and indicates the sanctity of this Mosques.

There are three mosques which could be traveled to:

Masjid Al Haram (in Makkah).
My Mosque (Prophet's Mosque in Madinah).
And Al Aqsa Mosque (in Jerusalem).

In another hadith, which means that the prayers in the Mosque in Makkah is equal to hundred thousand prayers (in its rewards) in any other Mosque except the Prophet's Mosque, where in the prayers there are equal to one thousand prayers, and the prayers in Al Aqsa Mosque in Jerusalem equals to five hundred - to a prayer in another mosque in the world (100.000 - 1000 - 500).

The Holy Mosque in Makkah - by day

Full with Muslims offering their prayers

View at night

Prophet's Mosque in Madinah

A view of the Prophets Mosque in Madina. Under the green dome is the tomb of the prophet and also the graves of his friends and companions Abu-Bakr and Omer.

THE PROPHET'S MOSQUE IN MADINAH:

When the Prophet of Islam migrated to Madinah he built his house in the middle of the town on a peace of land which he bought. Besides and adjacent to his house he built the mosque where he lead the prayers, and gave sermons.

Later on this mosque became his meeting place where he received the tribal leaders, the emissaries and representative and ambassadors of other countries. In this mosque he would also hold council with his companions and all the people who would come to visit him or to pray and worship in this mosque.

The mosque was built with mud and clay, and the roof was covered with the Palm or date tree leaves and branches.

In the beginning of Islam the Qibla or the direction of prayers was towards the Al Aqsa Mosque in the north, but in the second year (AH) in the month of Sha'ban, the revelation came to change the Qibla towards the Ka'abah in Makkah . The Prophet was most delighted with this change. So from that time all Mosques and all Muslims throughout the world would face towards the Ka'abah in Makkah, while offering their prayers.

With the increase of the number of the believers accepting and joining Islam this mosque has become small and the need for its expansion arose. So the Prophets companion Othman ibn Affan bought the land besides it for the mosque to be expanded, and it was made fairly big.

Since that time, about 1425years, the Prophets mosque received the required care and attention and has been expanded rebuilt and renovated continually until the present time.

It had its share of building through various Islamic Ca liphs and rulers from Banu Omaya, Abbasid, Fatimia and the Turkish Otoman rule - until the present day Saudi Government with all its rulers, until the final or recent and biggest and most modern expansion and construction in the era of King Fahd, the custodian of the two holy mosques - This recent expansion made it the second largest mosque after the Holy Mosque in Makkah.

In this Mosque Prophet Mohammed (Peace be upon him) led the Prayers before was raised on the nocturnal journey.

The third Holy Mosque - Al Aqsa in Jerusalem

Jerusalem is one of the oldest cities in the world. It is in Palestine. It is the most revered and holy land after Makkah and Madinah. Because in this area were born and lived, and passed through and died, and buried are many prophets and Messengers of God. So its sanctity and holiness among the divine believers of different sects. They all revere and respect this land because all of them have their apostles or prophets who lived in this land. Jesus Christ (peace be upon him) was born in this area, and was raised to heaven from there.

For the Muslims it is also a holy place as Prophet *Mohammad* (peace be upon him and all the prophets and messengers of God) was there, one year before his migration to Madinah. One night in the month of Rajab he was brought to the Al Aqsa Mosque in Jerusalem from Makkah, and from there he was elevated and raised to the skies in heaven where he was given the command for his followers to offer and perform the five times prayers. It was all in a one night Journey, as it was mentioned in the Qur'an:

Glory be to Him who made His servant (*Mohammad*) go by night from the sacred Mosque (Makkah) to the further Mosque (Al Aqsa), whose surroundings We have blessed, that We will show him some of our signs (marvels). He (God) who hears all and knows all. { 17:01}

The Al Aqsa Mosque in Jerusalem was the first Qibla of Islam. In the beginning of Islam Muslims used to face the direction towards this Mosque to offer their prayers. But in the second year after migration to Madinah came the inspiration and command from Allah to change the Qibla direction towards The Ka'abah in Makkah.

{ 2:144} Verily, we have seen the turning of your (Mohammad's) face towards the heaven. Surely. We shall turn you to a Qiblah (prayer direction) that shall

please you, so turn your face in the direction of Al Masjid Al Haram

(The Holy Mosque in Makkah). And where-ever you people are, turn your faces (in prayer) in this direction. Those to whom The Scriptures were given know this to be the truth from their Lord. And Allah is not unaware of what they do. (2:144)

In the year 15 (AH) during the time of the 2nd Caliph Omer the city of Jerusalem, which was known as Elia, was under siege by Muslim Army. Eventually the Romans who were occupying this city gave up and offered to surrender but only to the hands of Omer, because he was known for his Justice. Omer came here from Madinah and an agreement was drawn and signed by Omer who gave all the inhabitants the peace and protection and the safety of their dwellings, and for the ones who would like to leave the city a safe passage with all their belongings, were allowed.

Abdul Malik ibn Marwan a Banu Omayya Caliph or ruler, built a big glittering dome above the rock from which Prophet *Mohammad* (peace be upon him) was elevated to heaven. The Rock Dome was built on the north side of the Aqsa Mosque. But in 490 AH (1100 AD) Jerusalem was taken away from the Abbasid Muslim Dynasty.

In the year 583 (AH) about (1200 AD) it was again freed by Salahuddin Al Ayubi from the Roman invaders and was restored to the Muslim rule.

THE MARVELS OF THE HOUSES OF GOD:

When we see the Kaabah and the two holy Mosques and all the other mosque's or houses of God which were built for worship, we find that it was built small and simple in the beginning, but with the passage of time and throughout the ages it became bigger and splendid monuments. It does receive all the attention all the times from believers every where who would not only do maintain these places of religious importance and worship, but also add to it their own decorations and expansion required, according to the time they live in, and the civilization and architectural culture of their time.

Most important fact about the houses of God is that in it people feel the security, inner serenity and selfcontent. Besides doing the worshipping, they get the urge and desire to do good deeds for themselves and for their fellow humans when they leave the Mosque.

The Dome of Rock from over which Prophet Mohammed (peace be upon him) ascended and raised to heaven in the nocturnal night journey. The Dome of Rock is in the courtyard of the Al Aqsah mosque, in Jerusalem.

THE CUSTODIANS OF THE TWO HOLY MOSQUES:

King Fahd:

Whenever the two great holy mosques are mentioned, the name of King Fahad of Saudi Arabia comes to mind, His name will go into history as one of the Muslim rulers who have contributed highly in the building and expansion of these two holy mosques, besides many other mosques he built around the world.

King Fahd is the fifth ruler of Saudi Arabia in succession after his father King Abdul Aziz, and brothers King Saud, King Faisal and King Khaled.

He took office in the year 1400 Hijri (AH) (1980 AD). Shortly after he became King, he denounced the title of "His Majesty" preceding his position as the King, and announced himself as the servant (or the custodian) of the two holy mosques and decreed it to be used as his official title. He became the first Muslim ruler in the history to use this title officially. And In times to come he proved himself to be worthy of this most noble title in the Muslim world.

As the servant or (the custodian) of the two holy mosques; King Fahad made the biggest expansion, of these two holy mosques in history. The finest technology, material and craftsmen were put and employed in the development of these two holy mosques.

At the same time, the old buildings of these two holy mosques, which were built by the earlier era were preserved and kept, after going through a complete repair and renovation process, especially the buildings which were built during the Othman's Turkish rule of Arabia.

He also expanded and renovated the first Mosque built in Islam in the Quba'a Area of Madinah.

The most important recent work is the complete reconstruction and renovation of the Holy Kaabah in 1419 hijri (1999 AD). As such he became the 12th builder in history of mankind who built, rebuilt or renovated the Ka'abah, The House of God, The Ka'abah.

He also built many Mosques around the world and built schools along with those mosques.

Among the many great works and accomplishments to serve his country and Islam, King Fahd has established a big and huge printing and publishing complex in Al Madinah - the Prophet's city in Saudi Arabia. This complex is dedicated to the printing and publishing of the holy Qur'aan in its original form in Arabic, and also its translation and interpretation in many other languages. Millions of copies of the Holy Qur'an and prophets hadith (sayings and deeds of the prophet (peace be upon him), and Islamic publications from this press are distributed for free through out the world, seeking the blessings of Allah.

He was a philanthropist who knew no bounds or limits to help the needy and the poor whom he knew, or who he was informed about, or who may have contacted him from all over the world, without distinction or discrimination. The help would come in many ways and forms; be it funds or grants to complete education for the ones who could not get proper education outside the kingdom, or for treatment in hospitals, or financial help to the needy and the destitute. And the widows and the orphans.

King Fahad ibn Abdul Aziz died in the year 2005, at the age of 84, after a long illness. His name will be remembered in history as a great leader and humble king – for the great services and accomplishments he did for his country and for Islam and the humanity, all around the world.

King Abdullah:

King Abdullah bin Abdul Aziz is the 6th in succession of rulers in Saudi Arabia. He has taken the pledge of being the King in 2005 after the death of his brother King Fahd.

He also assumed the noble title of The Custodian of the two Holy Mosques instead of the usual title of "His Majesty" which is used by monarchs and Kings.

The first thing he did after his ascension as the king, he issued his orders for more expansions of the two holy Mosques. The most important part of his programme is to cover the large open areas in and around the two holy Mosques in Makkah and Madinah – with large sun-roofs/shades or umbrellas which will cover the open areas during the noon and after noon time to protect the pilgrims and worshippers from the scorching heat of the sun, especially in the Holy Mosque courtyard around the Ka'abah and it would be erected or built in such a way that it will cause no inconvenience and or hindrance to the pilgrims going around it while doing the Tawaf (circumbulation). And these huge umbrellas will be retracted during the evenings and night to give the place a natural atmosphere and feelings of open sky, after sunset.

The sun shade which was ordered by King Abdullah bin Abdul Aziz

(ARCHITECTURAL VIEW OF THE PROGRAMS OF SHADES TO BE ERECTED OVER THE KA'BAH AND THE COURTYARD OF HARAM MOSQUE IN MAKKAH)

WHO LEADS THE PRAYERS?

The Emam in the Mosques:

Mosques are built so that Muslims would pray together in congregations. The congregation in the mosque is led by an appointed leader who is called the Emam. He is chosen among the most learned and religious persons to lead the congregations. He should have a good knowledge of the rules and duties of his religion, Islam. He should know and remember most parts, preferably he should memorize and remember all the chapters of the Qur'an by heart. He should be a good reader with a good voice to recite the Qur'an. Because when it is read in nice and good voice, the Qur'an goes straight in the hearts and minds of the listeners, as against the one who does not recite well, and his bad voice is not greeted by the ears, save the heart and mind. So a good reader with a melodious voice to recite is more appropriate for an Emam, besides being of a good soul and character.

The Mouazin:

This is also an important job delivering the Azan or the call of prayers in its proper timings. The Mouazin rises on a high place or top of the mosques so that people from far away places can hear him. Eventually, and later on, a tower was made in the mosques for this purpose where the Mouazin can climb and do the prayer calls. The towers were developed as minarets and became a significant part of the mosques. Now a days the Audio system helps in extending the Azan to far away places It is an important job to be a mouazin, and a person with loud and melodious voice is a proper person for this noble job.

Bilal Al Habshi:

He is the first Mouazin in Islam. Bilal was appointed or designated as the caller for the prayers by Prophet *Mohammad* (peace be upon him). He was a black slave. He heard about *Mohammad* and his new religion, and was among the earlier persons who became Muslims in Makkah.

He found out that there is no discrimination or racism in Islam. When his masters knew about him accepting the religion of Islam, they were angered and outraged. They would not let their slave change from their religion without their permission. So they would beat him mercilessly; and force him to lie-down on his bare back on the ground in the middle of the day under the hot sun. They would also put a big stone on his chest, and ask him to renounce his new religion, which he would refuse. Abu Baker, *Mohammad's* closest friend in Makkah, who was also a wealthy trader saw this inhuman treatment of Bilal, he could not but intervene. He offered to buy this slave. His owner was happy to get rid of this useless slave for them, without losing his cost. So they sold him to Abu Bakar, who bought him happily, and took him to the Prophet. He became among the companions of the prophet. Because of his melodious and good voice, the Prophet delegated the job of Mouazin to Bilal. After the conquest of Makkah in the 8th year (AH) The Prophet along with his companions and followers entered the Kaabah. They cleaned it, and banished all the idols from within and around the Kaabah. Then the Prophet asked Bilal to climb on top of the Kaabah and do the Azan, which he did. It was a historical occasion and that was the turn over of things and the real beginning or advent of Islam. Prophet *Mohammad* entered Makkah without a fight, and the people who were his ardent enemies before his migration to Madinah now flocked in from every where to greet him as their leader, pledged their allegiance and accepted his religion.

WHAT IS AZAN?

Azan is the call for the believers, announcing to them, the time for prayers have entered. Because each prayer should be offered in its proper time, and each prayer has its time limit, The Azan advises of the beginning of that time. The prayers cannot be performed or offered before its designated time, so does the call or announcement cannot be made before that fixed time.

In the beginning Islam started slowly and secretly. The need for this call was not yet revealed or recognized. But later on in Madinah, when the Mosques were built, then the need for this call arose. There were discussions to find out a proper way or method to let the people know of the beginning of prayer times. Some of the companions saw in their dreams this call and the way it is done. So they told the Prophet about it, and because of its logic and substance, he approved it. And it became the official call for prayers. This is the way the Azan or the call for prayers are done five times a day:

Allaho Akbar, Allaho Akbar,	Twice
Ash-hado unla Ilaha Illa Allah	Twice
Ash-Hado Anna *Mohammad*an Rasool Allah	Twice
Haya ala Alsalat	Twice
Haya ala AlFalah	Twice
Allaho Akbar, Allaho Akbar - La ilaha Illa Allah	Twice

And its translation is as follows:

Allah is Great, Allah is Great	Twice
I testify that there is no God but Allah	Twice
I testify that *Mohammad* is His Messenger	Twice
Proceed for the prayers	Twice
Proceed for the success	Twice
Allah is Great	Twice
There is no God but Allah	Once

And this is the call for prayers which we hear five times a day from every Mosque all around the world. It is the call for righteousness. It is a call for the prosperity of mankind. It is the call for human solidarity.

CHAPTER
14

IMPORTANCE AND PREFERENCE
IN ISLAM

CONCEPT OF ISLAM:

Islam is not only a religion which people will embrace or accept just for the sake of it, to be known as Muslims. But it is a way of life that whoever accepts should also adhere to its teachings and comply with its rules and perform its duties and rituals faithfully.

A Muslim should be a hard working person who works sincerely for himself his family and society with value and pride. A Muslim should be clean, sincere, truthful and trustworthy.

There are many aspects of life which are clearly defined that if a believer would follow he would not only be on the safe side - but he would be beneficial to himself, his family and the society at large.

Islam is a way of life that considers the right path, and differentiates between the right and wrong and opts logically for the right and good deeds and sincerely tries to avoid the wrong and bad deeds and sayings.

Some of these important aspects are mentioned and explained here plainly and simply.

JUSTICE IN ISLAM:

Islam came in a time when justice was not known. There was no social justice available. Girls were used to be buried alive because of shame or poverty. Women had no right and the poor were ill treated.

In such a chaotic time Islam came to organize the dealings between human beings based on justice, so that people can live in peace and harmony and not on oppression and depression.

It emphasizes on the equal rights of people regardless of their race - color or creed. To obtain this objective Islam emphasizes on justice and it became one of its main and primary objectives to impose and implement justice among people in the society.

Without justice people will live the law of the jungle, where the mighty and wealthy would oppress the weak and the poor and there would be no one who would dare to help the wretched or humble.

So, it had setup a court system which would deal in everyday matters of justice. Judges are appointed according to their knowledge of Islamic law and concept, intelligence and pietism.

In the beginning Prophet *Mohammad* (peace be upon him) himself used to govern and judge between the people in Madinah and when the Islamic state started to expand, he assigned pious and religious persons and sent them to open court and look into the matters of justice among people in other cities and places, emphasizing on them to do justice fairly, while appointing them.

Justice should be done without delay - because delay in Justice to the rightful is equal to injustice. Also justice shall be done without regard to name or fame, or wealth and might of the opponents. It is based and done strictly on the evidence and circumstances available without coercion, and judges should be Just and impartial while doing their job. Judges in courts have full freedom to perform their duties without coercion and pressure from anyone. Justice is to all and must be carried rightly, as it is for everyone.

At the time of the Prophet a woman who was under trial for stealing was being Judged by the Prophet himself, when it was recommended by some of the relatives to be lenient on her. This made the Prophet angry and he denounced such matters by saying (which means) that "why people would recommend for the wealthy and known people in such matters" He swore that even if his own daughter (Fatima) was guilty of such a crime he would carry out justice by punishing her accordingly –(cutting her hand in this case). This is the epitome of justice in Islam. No favoritism.

Judges should be just and impartial, and they should be keen to find and obtain the truth and do justice in their courts. Islam does not accept the sayings which says, the law does not protect the simple minded. The law should protect the right of everyone regardless if they are simple minded or smart persons.

In one of the Prophet's sayings he described the judges in three categories. Saying: two judges belong in hell, and one judge belongs in heaven.

A judge who does not know, and does not try to find out the truth, and then delivers his judgment based on incorrect knowledge and information - he belongs in hell.

A judge who knows the truth and then delivers the judgment incorrectly or unjustly, he also belongs in hell .

A judge who looks for and seeks the truth and delivers his judgment fairly according to good justice - he belongs in heaven.

This is the understanding of the Prophet's sayings which clearly emphasizes on the neat, clean and just judgments which are the back-bone and strong structure of every society. Justice done in time and with true findings is justice well done. And justice well done is justice well served. Delay in meeting out justice is also equal to injustice.

Also there is a saying of the Prophet which means "who ever sees a detestable thing (abominable act - atrocity etc.) he should change (or alter) it by his (own) hands, or by his tongue (sayings), or by his heart (inside feelings) and that is the weakest of faith."

In this saying it is emphasized on people that who so ever sees wrong doings or detestable acts being done should try to correct it by all means possible. By changing it personally if he can, or asking authorities, by saying and asking for help to do the changes - or at least should detest this act inside himself - if he cannot do the other two things or complain.

The Judge is a forceful authority who can change detestable acts through his Just judgments. And to have proper justice Islam also deplores and condemns false testimony.

INJUSTICE:

Injustice is the main cause of problems in any society. It starts at home when a father or the parents intentionally favor some of their children without any valid or acceptable physical or psychological reasons, and play hard on the others. With this wrong and unjust attitude they make the ones who were let out become indignant, and violent.

They will grow disliking their parents and hate their brothers or sisters who unjustly became the favored group of their parents. This makes the base for family feuds, and social injustice. The fight erupts after the demise of these unjust parents or at anytime regardless.

In one occasion a companion of Prophet came and asked him to testify that he gave a gift to one of his sons. The Prophet asked him if he had given similar gifts to his other children. The person replied that he did not. The Prophet then refused to testify for this and he told the person that he should be treating all his children equally - and should not discriminate between them.

The feeling of injustice becomes strong and the hate becomes stronger when some one by force and with the aid and help of some-one stronger or with authority like the patriarch of the family or clan, receives or gets things which belongs to the other's and have it to himself without any right to it what so ever. Hence, the oppressed one will fight for his belongings or his rights.

The parents in this case do accuse the neglected or oppressed ones of being rude and aggressive. They forget that they were and are the cause of this wild or unpleasant situation.

Once the cause of this wrong situation is removed or corrected or at least an explanation or a replacement is given to consolidate the mistake will make the big difference between human's, and will calm down the situation if it did not make it pleasant.

This and other acts of unjust favoritism also become the reason for jealousy and animosity among people in the society. It makes dents and holes in the society's fiber. People will not work positively especially the oppressed ones - because of the heavy burden of oppression on their mind and soul. Also the one's who were unjustly favored would not work and perform properly. Because in the first place they may not be eligible or capable or qualified of doing that job, and secondly they would feel that no one would question them for the ineptitude or negligence they may do in their job, and also that they are the chosen one for any place or position - without having the necessary qualification or experience, because of their favored relations.

This is why it is explained in the interpretation of the verse regarding the daughters of the old man (Prophet Shoaib) when they asked their father to employ Moses (peace be upon him) in their service. They found out two good features that they pleaded their father to hire him for: One that he was strong (He alone did fetch the water from the well for them and carried it tirelessly to their house), and the second reason is that he was trustworthy.(he did not peek or sneak on them while helping them, and when he was asked to go and see their father.)

"And said one of them' O my father hire him verily, the best of men for you to hire is the strong and trustworthy." { 28:26}

Scholars interpret this verse in the general terms of hiring the right person in the right place, and that he should know his job well and he must be trustworthy. There are two important conditions to place someone or appoint him on to a job that is, that the person is eligible and qualified and that he is sincere and trustworthy.

Also there is a Hadith of the prophet which means that who so ever (a ruler) who appoints (or employ) someone in a position to serve the people while there are other persons more qualified than him available and were not given the chance - will not smell the fragrance of heaven or paradise.

Appointing the right person in the right place and giving the people their right dues is an important message of Islam. It is an important aspect of running the peoples affair by putting knowledgeable and trust-worthy people to manage important positions. It helps in the smooth administration and fair operations of any governmental or corporate facility. Placing an ill equipped in knowledge and untrustworthy person, to run public affairs is an unjust affair according to Islamic perspective.

MUFTI (OR FORMAL RELIGIOUS ADVISOR):

The Mufti is a learned religious scholar who delivers or provides FATWA or formal advisories on matters of concern to the people in light of the religion and give counsel on religious matters. He should be well educated and well versed in religious subjects. He has learned and memorized the Holy Qur'an by heart. He has studied, learned and understood the Hadith or the Sayings and deeds of Prophet *Mohammad* (peace be upon him). And he has the sense of understanding, visualizing and deduction of the Right and Wrong. He would advise and explain the religious matters correctly, as humanly possible, according to his knowledge.

Because of their vast knowledge and well understanding of their religion some of these Mufti's are appointed as official religious Advisors (MUFTI) in Muslim countries, and they are well respected in their communities, as this is a great position they occupied.

Some of the scholars or religious advisors may differ in their opinion or answers to certain matters according to their learning Schools or their understanding of the matter and the way it is put to them. But generally they all agree on the basis and basics of their religion, Islam.

WOMEN

In the pagan era in Arabia, and before the advent of Islam women's place was the lowest in the society, she was literally treated like a down cast or a slave. When a person is told that a baby girl was born in his house he feels ashamed, and thinks that a catastrophe happened to him. There are many who buried their young daughters alive without a sign of remorse or a degree of kindness and mercy.

Even in today's world there are many societies where women are oppressed and treated badly. They still think and feel the girl in their house hold as a burden at the least. Because when the time comes for her to get married her parents have to take the full brunt of her dowry which they have to pay to the husband, and to furnish his house fully. Otherwise their daughter will be ill treated by him and his family for the rest of her life - if they would spare it. In Islam it is the husband who has to arrange for the house and furnish it and pay the dowry to the bride, and not vice-versa.

WOMEN IN ISLAM:

All those things are changed since Islam came. It raised the status of women to the highest level any society could give her accordingly. Her high place in society is recognized and established as the mother, wife, sister and daughter. She is to be well treated; respected, loved and taken care of.

As a Mother:

the women have the highest place in their house hold. All her children must treat her with love and respect. Her wishes are their command. They should not disobey or displease her. Because Prophet *Mohammad* emphasized many a times of the sanctity of the mother, and warned his followers, not to be unkind to her. In one of the Hadith the Prophet says which means the "heaven lies under the feet of the mothers."

In another instance the Prophet was asked by some one as to who is more entitled to his act of kindness and gratitude (his father or his mother?). To which the Prophet replied your Mother. When asked who else, again the Prophet said your Mother. The Prophet three times repeated to the enquirer that his Mother is the one entitled for the acts of kindness and gratitude, And on the fourth time he said "Your father". This shows how Islam emphasized on the need to respect, love and acts of kindness to be given to the Mother. Because she is the one who took the brunt of raising the child from pregnancy until the birth and the breast feeding and pampering as a baby and taking good care as a child until one becomes old enough to stand his ground and becomes a person of some value in the society. She does deserve to be treated very well with all the kindness especially when she becomes old.

As a Wife; Islam urges for the good treatment of women, and they should be treated equally and with kindness, love and care by her husband. She also should treat him kindly and with respect and love. She is the dean of the household. Same good treatment goes for the sisters, and daughters who should be treated as their brothers or the sons should be treated.

Women in Islam have the right of ownership. Whatever she inherits is hers and she is free to spend and use it as she pleases and deems fit. She does not have to foot the bills in her household, because that part is the responsibility of the husband. If she voluntarily spends or helps in this, it is her prerogative, and good gesture, and she is not obliged to do so.

Only for this reason she gets half the share of her brothers in inheritance. Because all the spending of a house hold is the responsibility of the man, and the women is free from this burden. Her brothers in this case are shouldering the responsibilities of their wives and house-hold, while she does not have those responsibilities.

Women generally are absolved from doing work outside the house as most of the outside works are done by men. Men are responsible to finance, and support all the house hold needs. Women does the house hold chores, and take care of her children and help in their up-bringing. And bring-up her children to be useful persons and respectful members of society, which by itself is great responsibility.

Women are to be treated as jewels and protected until she finds the right person to marry. When after her marriage she would have her own children, she has the right, 'and deserves to be respected and loved and obeyed by her children for being such a clean and pious women.

MARRIAGE IN ISLAM:

The purpose of marriage is to have a new family in the society. It is to continue the natural life line or cycle of the people, and to build and populate or rehabilitate the world on this planet. The new family through the marriage becomes a new entity and grows up to become a big family in due time, when they will have their own children to take care of. These children eventually will have their own brothers, sisters, cousins, aunts and uncles, and so on. It becomes an independent family in the society. It is a sacred bondage between a man and a woman, and it is performed under the religious system or social laws, which every one respects. It is a sacred bondage and holy partnership between a man and a women, their families, tribes and the societies they live in, and which becomes closer through this social act of marriage. It makes different families likes each other and it brings love and respect among them through the marriage of one of their family member. When a couple (a man & a women) are married, they immediately finds themselves becoming a member of each others family, and the circle of their relatives and loved ones suddenly becomes greater and bigger.

This is a normal and happy life system, and it is completely different from the way of life of couples living together outside the wedding or marriage system. The extra-marital, or unmarried couple living together is unacceptable in all religions. Islam also prohibits this kind of living and deems it as a great sin. Even in to-day's open or permissive societies in the world married couples are eyed with envy, and receives a respectful and warm welcome every where.

Like other religions in Islam also, marriage is conducted officially by an authorized and licensed official who is well-versed in the Islamic family law. The father or an authorized guardian of the bride will give away the bride, or consent on her behalf, in agreeing for this marriage. Besides the groom, two male witnesses also should be present in this official procedure.

During this procedure the groom will declare the amount of dowry he is giving to the bride. This dowry which has already been agreed upon earlier between the couple or their families, or offered during this procedure and which shall be stipulated in the marriage contract, becomes the property of the bride, and she will have the right to it, and use or spend it as she pleases. Counter and opposite to some cultural habit or taboo, in Islam the groom is responsible for the accommodations and proper furnishings of the house, and not the bride or her parents. The bride and her parents may chip in or share whatever they can voluntarily, if the groom is unable, and if they can help. This is a welcome situation to improve the new family relations. After this procedure the couple becomes husband and wife.

From now on the couple accepts the responsibility of each other, in sickness or in health, or in happiness and sorrow, or in any situation, until death do them part, or the agreement is terminated through divorce procedures.

There after follows the ceremony where all the family and friends gather to feast and felicitate the couple, and enjoy the festivities and the ceremony. This feast is called the WALIMA, and it is to announce the marriage of the couple and make it public. In the context of marriage, besides the rights they have on each other, both sides have some responsibilities also to make the marriage ongoing or worthwhile by doing their part of the deal sincerely and faithfully, so as to keep this marriage to continue on smoothly and peacefully. Another thing which will help in this institution is the love and kindness they show to each other, and the forgiveness any one of them would do to the other in case of wrongdoing or shortcoming, and try to help in undoing the shortcomings, kindly. They should recognize that man and women are built differently. Physically, mentally and emotionally they differ. But this difference is not for competing but to complete and compliment each other in their family affair.

The men in the family institution have big responsibilities of protecting their family and providing for them their livelihood and healthcare and its security. It is like every group has a leader, and every ship has a captain. And men in the family life are the leaders or captain. The women also have big responsibilities of keeping household assisting the husband and bringing-up the children. In the Qur'an it is mentioned thus:

"Men are in charge of women by virtue of what (qualities) Allah has given one over the other and for what they spend from their wealth (income). The righteous women are devoutly obedient, guarding (in the husband's absence) what Allah (would have them) guard .." (4:34) Al Nissa.

We should understand that in marriage the men and women are not in competition for the dominance of one over the other. Both the husband's and the wife's should take up their responsibilities seriously and carefully, taking into consideration the needs of each other, help and assist each other, and love and be kind to each other. This will make their home a heaven, in this world. Islam requires and encourages both to do their part of the deed, faithfully.

Although it is permissible and normal to marry within the family i.e.: cousins can marry cousins, The Prophet did encourage people to marry outside the family circle. This way the circle of family and friends becomes bigger and wider, and the relations in the society becomes closer and stronger. And in the Qur'an it is mentiond thus:

" O Mankind We (God) have created you from a male and a female, And made you into nations and tribes, that you may know one another, Indeed the most noble of you in the eyes of Allah, is the most righteous (most pious) among you. Indeed Allah is All Knowing (and) All Aware."

PLURALITY IN MARRIAGE:

Long time ago I was in a western country for study. I was young and unmarried then. I met a very nice gentleman, who was older then me. We became friends as we met often in the lobby of the small hotel we were staying.

One day he told me that he intended to visit the next town besides us. He said "I have my girl friend over there." He told me he will spend sometime there with her and that he will come back after the weekend.

Next day he surprised me when he called to tell me that he could not go to meet his girl friend because his wife came last night. She gave him a surprise visit, and he asked to see me this evening as usual.

That evening I invited him and his wife for dinner. His wife was also a nice and charming old lady. During our joyful dinner conversation she curiously asked me "Are you married"? I said "no I am not married, yet". Then my friend, her husband, asked me jokingly and with a big grin, "and how many wives are you going to have, when you get married"?.

I was really surprised with this change of course in our conversation, but then as it came to my mind I answered, "I may have four wives!" She almost choked with the shock and asked amazingly "Four wives?!!!" And we all were laughing.

Then I explained to them that Islam allows or permits men to marry more than one wife, and up to four wives maximum - at one time. I also explained that there is a permission here, and not a definite order or urge. And this permission is for necessity and with a strong condition. The condition is to treat all the wives in equal terms, which even the Qur'an emphasizes, that it is impossible to treat them so, equally. And I had to add that in this system it is the respect and integrity of the women that is upheld. Instead of being just a friend to serve him, and she may not have any right on him, but in marriage a woman will have her rights, her integrity and respect as a wife. It make no difference if she is the 1st or 2nd or 3rd or 4th wife. They all are in a marriage bindings, with all its merits and responsibilities.

Islam deals in reality, openness and truth. It does not promise women's lib or freedom which makes her a doll in the society and can be used or abused by false pretense. She is a free human being after all. Men also are not allowed to abuse the women and they should treat them with respect and dignity. And this permission is to avoid these wrong and false pretenses on both sides.

In this way, a person whose wife may not be able to bear children, and wishes and desires to have his own children, and/or his wife may be continually ill, or may not able to fulfill her marital obligations, and he can afford to marry another wife, he may use this permission. He does not have to divorce his first wife if she agrees to stay with him, without losing her status or rights. This way even the children of these wives will have their rights as the legitimate children, and will be equally eligible for inheritance of their father, and will not lose their position in the society. They all become sisters and brothers for each other, and are treated as such.

The man does not have to find a girl friend or a mistress in the dark! Also the women will have integrity and respect in the open world. Islam works for the betterment of society and does not allow wrong doings under false and wrong slogans and pretense.

DIVORCE:

Islam is a religion which was bestowed on human beings to help them live a harmonious and peaceful existence. It encompass and understand the needs and requirement's of human-beings, and have laws and regulations, if people adhere to, would help them in solving most of their problems in life.

In the previous subject, it is emphasized as how to maintain an honest and happy marriage. But alas! many things in life do not continue or work as we would like it to be. And some times in life sweet things may go sour, because of many reasons. Usually, we do not blame ourselves, and mostly we blame the other side even if it was our fault. This is human nature, which should be corrected. And therein comes the laws and regulations of societies and religions to interfere and correct the situations.

Unlike some religions or social misunderstandings which are against human nature, that enforce marriage to be everlasting and stipulate it "till death do us part" strongly. But   Islam consider it a relation or partnership which could and should be dissolved if it could not be resolved amicably through other cordial means, and when living together within this framework becomes impossible due to in-conciliatory situations where either or both the husband or thewife are unable to function or live properly with each other.

As the last and bitter remedy for this social malady Islam does allow the last alternative, which is the Divorce. Although it is per-missible and legitimate act, Islam does not encourage it, but allowed it as the final act after absolving all other acts of reconciliation. The Prophet have said which means that "The most hateful permissible act with Allah, is the Divorce." Even though it is an action which is permissible or Halal - God does not like it.

Since this permission is there, it should not be taken casually and misused. There are rules to be followed so that it is not taken for granted. People who are ignorant of Islamic rule imagine that it has a casual attitude towards divorce allowing it to happen as a word; i.e. when an angry husband says 'I divorce you'. Islam looks at divorce as a long process if it is to be done properly and according to Islamic procedure. The process of divorce begins with arbitration, as ordered by God Almighty in the Qura'an:

"If you have reason to fear that a breach may occur between a (married) couple, appoint an arbiter from his people and an arbiter from her people (an arbiter from each side). If both (the arbiter's) want to set things aright, God will bring about their reconciliation. God is All Knowing, All Aware". (Al Nissa - 35)

If arbitration fails, and divorce is inevitable, then it must be approached according to Islamic rule and its teachings.

Without going into full details of the divorce conditions and procedure in Islam, it is in short, the husband may divorce his wife two times consecutively , and in both the times he may renounce his action and return his wife back either by his sayings or actions, if she agrees. But after the third time the divorce is sealed for good, and permanently. Unless of course, the wife after the required waiting period of three months and 10days after her divorce, marries another person, and that person dies away or they were divorced due to their own circumstances, and unconditionally. Then the wife may return to her first husband if she is willing, and so desires, and with a new marriage contract and procedure, and a new dowry !

INHERITANCE IN ISLAM:

Prophet *Mohammad* (peace be upon him) once visited one of his companions Sa'ad bin Abi Waqas, who was sick. He was very pleased with this visit of the Prophet. He was seriously ill. He said to the Prophet asking for his permission, that he wants to give his wealth in charity before he dies. The Prophet told him that it was too much to give it all. He then said he would give half of it - to which the Prophet again said - that it was too much also. Then he asked if he may give one third, to which the Prophet reluctantly agreed, saying that one third also was still too much. The Prophet said (which means) that it is better to leave your dependents rich than leaving them poor asking or requiring help or charity from others, and leave them little or nothing.

Islam encourages that people would leave a will (better in writing, or verbally) to provide some part, however small it may be of their inheritance, to be given to some one in need and who is not an immediate family member and is not originally entitled for the inheritance or a dutiful servant, in compensation for their services or favors which they may have given to him during his lifetime. The inheritance is described in the holy Qur'an elaborately in the beginning passages in surat Al Nissa'a

The inheritance is generally divided among the immediate family members and direct descendants and dependents of the deceased - like the children, the parents and the spouse. And among the children the sons gets two shares against the daughters who would get one share, (She gets half of what her brother would receive.)

There comes a question in the minds of many people why the sons inherit double the share of the daughters, or how come the sisters receive half the shares in comparison with their brothers?

Muslims who believes in Allah whole heartedly and in His Prophet *Mohammad* (peace be upon him) would not ask any question as to 'why' when anything is decreed in the Holy Qur'an, and it is advised or explained to us by the Prophet. Instead we should say " indeed our Lord, we accept and obey all your commands." Because we believe in what ever is said in the Qur'an and we obey to all the commands in it, without questions regardless if we could understand the meanings or reasons behind it - because we know for sure and believe that Allah is the Best of Judges.

And to avoid any notions or wrong conclusions in the minds of the non believers, and also the ignorant, here we explain this situation thus: In Islam the men or the husbands are the providers and supporters of the their family members needs and requirements. As such all the house hold expenses and expenditures are their responsibility - and they have to foot the bills - all bills!

The woman or wife is absolved of this responsibility and whatever money or wealth she may have or receives as her inheritance does belong to her fully and she is not compelled to use it or any part of it for this purpose, paying the house hold bills !. She may give in as help - but that is her choice and prerogative. So, practically she will have a bigger share of inheritance then her brothers the men !, who have to shoulder the burden of their family. And in this way Islam justifies the help to the men in their inheritance. The men are even responsible for the welfare and expenses of their sisters if they have no husband to support them.

In this subject, there is a saying by the Prophet (no will is required for an heir). For example the children are the direct descendants of their Parents and thus they do not require a will as their rights have already been determined in the Qur'an and they are among the first in line to receive the inheritance from their parents. And as such they should not be barred or blocked from receiving their right which is already been described, through wrong or personal excuses Family members are eligible for inheritance according to their proximity in actual relationship and their shares also varies from person to person, as it is described in the Qur'an.

An important issue in the matter of inheritance is the debts of the deceased which should be clarified finalized and fully paid or absolved by the creditors before the inheritance is distributed among the heir apparent. Creditors of the deceased have precedence in obtaining their rights of actual outstanding loans, and not any interest or 'fees' (as usury or interest is prohibited in Islam), before the inheritors. And if there is nothing left by the deceased than we should ask them to forgive or forgo their claims, hoping to get more compensation of their good will and good deeds from Allah.

A note to the wise - Besides leaving enough and ample for your relatives and inheritors you should also invest as much as you can ((without depriving your relatives of their rights on you and your wealth) in long terms charities - like building orphanage, houses for the poor, sick and old people, leaving provision in the endowment funds also for other poor relatives who are not your legal inheritors and Making Charity hospitals etc etc. These investments you make in this world will be a great assets accumulating and waiting for you in the life after, and you will be richer even there. You will also receive the praise of God and His awards and bounties, and the majestic life of leisure in heaven.

And if you flounder your wealth in wrong doings instead, and did not leave anything for your inheritors as they have rights in your wealth, then you will arrive in the next life wretched and poor. You will find nothing waiting for you except misery, shame and sorrow.

That is not all - you will also be answering for all your wrong doings as well. And one of the questions a person would be ask is: How and where did you spend your wealth when you were alive. A wise person would not like to be in such a miserable situation which may derive severe punishment as well. Also his family members would be disappointed in him, and they may not pray for his well being in the life after death. They may curse him instead !. A nice and wise person would avoid this bad situation, and spend the wealth God have provided him with, in good and useful ways, and wisely.

HALAL AND HARAAM:

The things Muslims or followers of the religion of Islam are urged and encouraged to do are all the good deeds and sayings which comes in the category of "Halaal" (or permissible). The things which they are forbidden or prohibited to do are the bad deeds and sayings which is called "Haraam" or prohibitive.

There are two most commonly used words among the believers in Islam, and these words are of significant meaning and idioms among the Muslims. These words are Halal and Haraam:

HALAL:

The word Halal literally means legitimate and permissible - it also means legal or lawful and allowable. This word is used to differentiate between good things and bad things in our life. Good things, good food, good and pouise life style. No stealing, no cheating etc. The income by which we provide ourselves and our dependant's living, food and shelter should be clear, clean and lawful income. It should not be earned from unlawful deeds, like gambling, bribery, stealing etc etc. The food and drinks are among our daily life use, so it should be Halal

Another way to show and explain the meaning of this word is "Marriage". By being "married" the husband and wife are legally bound into companionship, and their relationship is considered Halal or legitimate, and the outcome of this relation will be the legitimate children.

Generally most of the things for Muslims are Halal (permissible), except where in a specific ordinance through the holy Qur'an or specified by the prophet through his sayings or deeds will make it Haraam. An example from the Qur'an for the food:

All good things have this day been made lawful to you. The food of those to whom the Scripture was given is lawful to you, and yours to them.

Lawful to you are the believing women and the virtous women from among those who were given the Scripture

before you, provided that you give them their dowries and live in honor with them, neither committing fornication nor taking them as mistresses.

He that denies the Faith shall gain nothing from his labors. In the world to come he shall have much to lose. [5:5]

(The Scriptures refered to in the above mentioned verses are the Tourah, or the Old Testament, and The Bible.)

This encourages Muslims to seek the Halal things in their daily life and discourages them from doing or eating Haraam.

HARAAM:

Haraam - means forbidden, prohibited, illegal, wrong doing ill-gotten unlawful and prohibitive etc. It is the opposite of Halal and doing it is sinful for believers, who are prohibited from adultery, alcoholic drinks, drugs, killings, stealing etc. these are the haraam actions. Also our food must not be bought through stolen or ill-gotten money like stealing, gambling - usury - bribery or obtained through any bad or loathsome deeds. They must not eat the meat of cattle killed or slaughtered in the name of anything but Allah. There are other kind of meats like the Swine or Pork, which is Haraam for Muslims and thus they must not eat any part of it and do not use the lard or any derivates from it.

The meat of cattles which are dedicated to any thing but God, when being slaughtered is considered Haraam. Also there is some type of meat which was not slaughtered properly or which was killed in an inhuman way or killed violently or met violent death. The meat of such animals or cattle is for bidden to eat as described in the Qur'an:

Muslims are forbidden carrion, blood, and the flesh of swine; also any flesh dedicated to any other diety or thing, except God. They are forbidden the flesh of strangled animals and of those beaten or gored to death; of those killed by a fall or mangled by beasts of prey (unless you make it clean and slaughter the injured animal yourself.); also of animals sacrificed to idols.

You are forbidden to settle disputes by consulting the Arrows. That is a pernicious practice. The unbelievers have this day abandoned all hope of vanquishing your religion. Have no fear of them: fear Me. This day I have perfected your religion for you and completed My favour to you. I have chosen Islam to be your faith. He that is constrained by hunger to eat of what is forbidden, not intending to commit sin, will find God forgiving and merciful. [5:3]

Halal and Haraam are not hollow or vague words. It have meanings which will make the difference between good and bad in the daily life use. Believers are advised to seek the good and clean things in life and abstain from known bad or evil things which have been declared prohibited or unlawful or impermissible which are described as Haraam.

{In the last sentence of the above verse there is an exceptional permission. When a person is in dire need to eat and has nothing else and there is no other choice, and in order to survive he may eat such meat, for survival only.

So in time of need and desperation a person may eat or drink what is otherwise for-bidden, - Only to survive and stay alive, and until he finds a better alternative!.}

When a person eats a nice and clean food, and dresses clean and neat cloths, it does affects his behavior. He becomes nice and good person, and he will be inclined to do good. His manners are firm but gentle. It is contrary to a person who does not care about his food from where it comes, or from what substance it is made of - or his dress is filthy or shabby - you can imagine how his behavior will be - he will be devilish!! His manners will be arrogant and rude.

THE NEIGHBORS:

One day a companion of the prophet (*Mohammad* Peace be upon him) was going to visit him, at his mosque. On the way he saw the Prophet peace be upon him was standing with someone who was talking to him for a long time. The companion stood aside and waited for the conversation to finish.

At last the person who was talking to the Prophet and kept him standing for such a long time finished his conversation and went. The companion of the Prophet was relieved and said "Oh Prophet of Allah, I was so much worried that you may have got tired standing with the person who was with you". The Prophet asked, you saw him, did you know who he was? He said yes I saw him but I do not know who he was. The Prophet then told him, that was the Arch Angel Gabriel, who came in a human form, to emphasize the importance of good treatment of the neighbors and who was emphasizing so much on the matter that the Prophet thought he may make the neighbors the receivers of the will of inheritance. So good neighbors are an asset in any society. Islam emphasizes on this good neighborly attitude, and emphasize on the people to be good neighbors.

Muslims must help their neighbors who are in need. They should visit each other and be friendly. Sometimes neighbors may be more beneficial then your own relatives because they are near-by and can give a helping hand quickly. Neighbors should be friendly, and they should not spy on each other, or propagate the shortcomings of each, if there is any. In a Hadith or saying of the Prophet (peace be upon him) which means, that no one of you is a believer (Muslim) whose neighbors are not safe from his bad and wrong doings.

And in another Hadith the Prophet (peace be upon him) says which means, "No one is a true believer who knows that his neighbors sleep hungry (they have no food), and you sleep with a full stomach". We are urged to feed our neighbors, if we know that they do not have food to eat, and we have food we can share!

ORPHANS:

Orphans are the children who may have lost either or both of their parents in their early age as infants and small children. Islam protects and maintains the rights of the orphans, for a good care.

Prophet of Islam *Mohammad* (peace be upon him)himself was an orphan, when he was born. His father Abdullah ibn Abdul Muttalib died before *Mohammad* was born. And his Mother Amna bint Wahb died when he was a child of five years. He was taken into the custody of his grandfather Abdul Muttalib, who loved him and took good care of him. He was eight years old when his grand father also died. Then his uncle Abu Taleb took him in his household and took care of him, so he know the pain of losing parents, and be deprived of their love and care.

Prophet of Islam said that which means "who ever sponsors (take care) of an orphan he will be with me (in heaven) like this " and he indicated with his two fingers, the index finger and the one besides it (the one beside the other, or together). This is a good news and omen and clear indication that the one's who would take good care of the orphan's will be the Prophet's companion in heaven. So, why should any believer lose this great opportunity to go to heaven, after death?!!! and be with the Prophet there, as he indicated and prophesized. He also said that which means, "Whoever places his hand with kindness on an orphan's head, he will be blessed by Allah as much as the number of hair on the (orphan's) head". So taking care of orphans is among the great charities and good deeds a person can do for his own good.

EATING THE INHERITANCE OF ORPHANS:

In the Qur'an it is mentioned:-

> **"Those that devour (eat up) the property (belongings) of Orphans unjustly (by oppression). They are going to eat fire in their stomach and they will be burned in a blazing fire."**
> { 4:10}

The people who are entrusted the guardianship of the orphans, and who would misuse that trust, and eat the inheritance of the orphans, are severely warned that they will be eating fire in their stomach, in their eternal life after death. Instead of honoring this trust and keeping the interest and welfare of their protégé in their consideration, they flounder their money and eat it up or keep it for themselves. Those are the people who were described in such a heinous way, and who would be punished so severely.

Orphans should be treated well and their belongings should be protected until such time that they became adults and can run their own affairs sensibly, then they are given their share of the inheritance without being eaten or used unjustly or floundered by their appointed guardians or administrators.

THE ISLAMIC VIEW OF ADOPTION:

Long before Prophet *Mohammad* (peace be upon him) began to receive any revelations, i.e. before prophet hood, he adopted Zayd ibn Harithah who was a slave given to him by his wife Khadeejah, when they were married. The Prophet never owned a slave for any length of time., He released Zayd from slavery and adopted him as his own son. From that time onward, Zayd was known as Zayd the son of *Mohammad*. This continued to be the case until the opening of Surah 33, Al-Ahzab, was revealed stating the categorical prohibition of adoption. It states:

He (i.e, God) has not made your adopted sons your real sons. This is only a word you utter with your mouths while God says only the truth and guides to the right path. Call them after their real fathers: for that is fairer in God's sight. If you do not know their real fathers, then they are your brethren in faith and servants. No blame shall be attached to you if you make a mistake. But (blame shall be attached) with

regard to that which you do deliberately. God is all-knowing, wise. (33:4 - 5)

These verses make it clear that adoption, in the sense of taking a child into a family and making him a son or daughter of that family, is not permissible in Islam. Zayd reverted to his original name as Zayd ibn Harithah, and was no longer called Zayd ibn *Mohammad*.

The reason for this prohibition is the fact that claiming a child as one's own through adoption is false, while Islam insists on truth. This is clear in the quoted verses that describe adoption in the sense mentioned as (a word you utter with your mouths.). Therefore, adherence to the truth is essential:

Having said that, we should remember that Islam attaches great importance to looking after orphans and giving them a proper upbringing. Any family that looks after an orphan, or an abandoned child, will be richly rewarded by God. The same applies to the sponsoring of an orphan child's upbringing and education as organized these days by a number of Islamic charities in deprived areas. This is done through giving a regular contribution. The child remains with its family, but receives what ensures for it a good upbringing. This is a compassionate act for which God gives very rich rewards. The Prophet says: (I will be in heaven with an orphan's sponsor like this – and he indicated with his two fingers.) This means that a person who brings up an orphan will have a rank in heaven very close to that of the Prophet. There can be no richer reward.

Adoption: As much as it emphasizes the need for protection and the right of orphans for a good care in a home where they would be brought up in a family atmosphere, Islam does not permit adoption in its entirety.

It differentiates between the human need of a child who needs the love and protection, and the emotional zeal to give it what is not required. It urges the society to take good care of the orphan within a family atmosphere. And instead of giving it a new identity, Islam protects the identity of the orphan itself.

Islam urges its members to do all the good and kindly deed of taking care of an orphan child and provide it with all that it needs. At the same time it emphasize that there is a limit to this human care. And that limit is to understand and maintain, that this is not your own child. That is a child which belongs to some other family, and it should have the right to keep its own identity, and should not be deprived of its family name and identity.

Islam urges its members to take good care of the orphan child; and treat them as well as you treat your own children. When they grow up send them to school, give them good education until they are grown-ups and are strong enough and prepared to enter life activity on their own. Find good work for them, and if they have inheritance in your custody give it to them, when you know that they can take care of themselves.

Islam also maintains that you must not take their family names from them and give them yours. They may have their own family line or ancestral linage. This is neither your right to do so, and nor their right for a new title. The ones who would have full claim of this right are your own children and relatives. You should not deprive your own children of their right by giving it to a stranger in your family, and they are not obliged to share it with anyone outside their household. When orphan grow older and strong enough, they are not considered orphans anymore, you could marry with them and they may marry within your family.

CHAPTER
15

VARIOUS OTHER ASPECTS OF ISLAM

The Islamic Calendar:

Like any other society or religion, Muslims also have their own calendar which they have adopted, and would adhere to strictly. This calendar was started and adopted at the time of the second Caliph of Islam Omer ibn AlKhatab, when he felt that the need to keep record of the events happening after the migration of the Muslims from Makkah and established their state in Madinah, which was in the year 622 AD, the year the prophet migrated. That became the first year for the Muslims, and this calendar is called After the Hijrah (AH) - or after the migration .

The basis of the Hijri or Islamic Calendar is the sighting of the birth of the moon in the beginning of every month, when it appeaears as a thin line or crescent in the sky, in the evening immediately after sunset. This is the sign of the beginning of the first day of the month. And this lunar movement or cycle of the month is repeated every 29 or 30 days.

The sighting of the beginning of the moon is an important mission. Muslim's are encouraged to look for and observe the sighting of the moon. When they see it clearly, they should testify and vouch for the observance and sighting of the beginning or the birth of crescent moon, Because with this sighting which at least two Muslim persons would testify to or vouch for, starts a new month, and so does the duties and obligations of the month starts with it. Like the month of Ramadan, when Muslims should observe its tradition and keep fasting and offering the required prayers

And so does the festivities of Eid would start when any person would testify that he saw the beginning of the moon, at the end of Ramadan, and thus the fasting ends and the festivities begins next day.

A very important aspect of sighting the beginning of the moon at the beginning of the month is to know and determine the most important day of the year. It is the day when the pilgrims should gather in Arafat for performing Hajj, which is on the 9thday of Dhul Hajj.

When the moon's beginning is not being sighted because of a cloudy day or any other weather reason, the month is completed as thirty days, after which the next month starts, as being directed by the Prophet of Islam Peace be upon him.

ANY SECRECY IN ISLAM:

Islam is an open religion. It does not have any secret clause, conditions or teachings. It does not have secret books, it is based on the only book which was first being revealed about 1438 Years ago, The Holy Qur'an. And the teachings and saying of its prophet *Mohammad* (peace be upon him) who through his open deeds and sayings taught his followers the correct way to worship God, and the correct way to offer prayers and perform the required duties of Islam, openly.

Also there are no secret rituals in Islam. Millions of people throughout the world could watch in their TV's how prayers and worships are performed by Muslims in the three Holiest Mosques of Islam, in Makkah, Madinah and Jerusalem, or in any other Islamic mosques around the world.

Islam is an open invitation to each and every one. It does not stop or refuse any one to join or embrace Islam. Also it does not compels anyone to join it by force, either. If a person believes in Islam and likes to join and becomes a Muslim, it is simple. He must believe in the first and foremost of its principles. He must believe in Allah as The God and the only God there is, and believe that *Mohammad* (peace be upon him) is His messenger. And then follow and adhere to the other rules and principles of Islam, and offer the prayers, and perform the required rituals, and abstain from wrong doings.

By believing and accepting the first principle, he becomes a muslim. He wins himself from whatever uneasy or harsh outcome that could be waiting for him in the next life, after death. And if a person does not want to believe in what he sees clearly in this life, and instead closes his eyes, or refuses the call of true faith, then he is the looser - and he may expect whatever waiting for him after death.

Islam does not contradict the divine and heavenly religions which came before it. Instead, it completes and compliments their teachings. And Prophet *Mohammad* (peace be upon him) as the last and final of the messengers of God, brought the final revelations and complete revisions in the belief of humanity.

From the Islam beginning the prophet of Islam was advised that his duty was to announce and propagate and not force or persuad, which he did dutifully, and God Himself will accomplish the rest. God will guide those who wishes to see the light and be guided. God also tells His Messenger, Prophet *Mohammad* (peace be upon him), who was sad that his own uncle Abu-Taleb did not accept the new belief since its beginning and did not become Muslim until he died. So Allah tells his prophet in the Qur'an;:

(you are not the one who would (usher) / guides whom you like, But Allah who will guide whom ever wishes so.)

Obligatory (Fardh) & voluntary (Sunnah) Worships:

There are two forms of worshipping in Islam. The Obligatory form which is called the Fardh, and it is part and parcel of the Principles of the faith of Islam. The other is the Non Obligatory worships which are known as Sunnah. These two forms of prayers and worships are similar in its ways of doing, and being performed.

The first one, The Fardh or Obligatory, is more important, as it is the mandatory or obligatory offerings of prayers which was designated and ordained by Allah for the Muslims to do.

FARDH: is the obligatory worship and prayers, and duty to observe and perform. Like the five times of Prayers during the day and night, and the Fasting being observed during the month of Ramadan. By obeying and performing their obligatory duties Muslims show their commitment and acceptance of the principles of Islam. All Obligatory Prayers and Rituals were ordained by Allah upon the Prophet to be conveyed to his followers, which he faithfully did. The Prophet has also explained how these rituals and prayers were to be observed and performed.

And if they do not observe or perform the stipulated duties they will incur the displeasure of Allah, and may expect His Punishments in this life and or in the life-after. Also, by not adhering to, and not performing the ordained Obligatory rituals and duties intentionally, a Muslim may be deprived of his status as a Muslim and he becomes an outcast and will deprive himself the blessing of Allah, and derives his wrath instead.

SUNNAH: is to follow the sayings and deeds of Prophet *Mohammad* (Peace be upon him). The extra and non-ordained prayers which he observed during his lifetime are also called The Sunnah. The Prophet used to observe voluntary prayers regularly. One night his wife Lady Khadija was so concerned when she saw his feet became swollen while he was offering voluntary prayers. She asked him anxiously "Why do you pray so much O Prophet of Allah, while Allah Has Forgiven you your past and the future ?" To which the Propet replied "Shouldn't I (then) be a thankful (grateful) Servant?"

The Sunnah are The Non Obligatory worships and voluntary Prayers which has been observed by the Prophet himself - and which he has described and made desirous to his followers,. These rituals are observed and performed voluntarily, following the footsteps and sayings of the Prophet. When it is performed or observed by Muslims it incur abundant Favors and Blessings of Allah. But when it is not performed or observed, it does not incur any displeasure or punishment thereto, because these are voluntary prayers and are not obligatory. Voluntary prayers may be offered as much as one can perform, and without obligations.

Sunnah worships and prayers do not replace The Fardh, but it does compliment and complete it. It adjusts and repairs the inadvertent mistakes and /or omissions incurred in the obligatory prayers which may have occured un-intentionally. In one of the Prophets Sayings which means :"When I ordain anything on you, observe from it whatever possible for you to do. And when I forbid you from doing anything you should abstain from doing that". And on another occasion the Prophet says, and which means : I have left with you (two things) which if you adhere to, you would never go astray, The Book of Allah (The Qur'an), and my way of life (Sunnah)". Some of these Sunnah Prayers were stressed upon by the Prophet himself, and he observed and did it regularly. These are known as Sunnah Mu'akkadh, like the two voluntary Rak'at,s he used to perform before the Fajr(Morning) Prayers, the two after Maghreb(after Sunset), and the Witr (Odd numbered) rak'ats after Isha (Night) Prayers.

THE FESTIVALS IN ISLAM:

There are two special occasions of festivities in Islam:

Eid Al Fitr:

This is the day after the month of Ramadan ends. It is the day Muslims around the world thanks Allah for his blessings during the month of Ramadan and for enabling Then to perform the rituals of fasting throughout the day, praying and worshipping in the night, offering charities and doing good deeds throughout the holy month, and abstaining from wrong doings.

It starts with the prayers on Eid day after the sunrise when every one, especially the women and children wear their fancy and best dresses while going to offer Eid prayer in congregation, in the main mosque of the city or in an open ground prepared for this purpose, where most of the people come for congregation, along with all the high officials and dignitaries. After the Eid prayers people felicitate each other, their relatives and loved ones. The celebration goes on for four days.

Eid Al Adha:

This is celebrated on the 10th day of Dhul Hajj (the month of Hajj). This is different from Eid Al Fitr. It is also for four days, and starts with Eid prayers on the first day. After the prayers the head of the family of each house hold would sacrifice cattle. A sheep or a goat or a cow or camel according to the status of the family. And this sacrifice can also be done during the next three days. This ritual of sacrifice of the cattle is to follow the example and guidance of Prophet Ibrahim (peace be upon him) who in his dreams was ordered to sacrifice his son Ismail near Makkah, and he did not be-lie the dream but accepted the command, and when he was ready to sacrifice his son God accepted his initiative, and his son was saved and a sheep was sacrified in his place.

RACISM:

Islam does not accept racism in any form. There is no difference between black and white or Asian and European or Chinese and African. You can see them all standing in one line in the mosque worshiping Allah together. In the sight of God all humans are equal except in their deeds. There is no discrimination among people because of their color or creed, in Islam. The best of them is the most righteous and pious person. They may live together; marry into each other without racism or apartheid. And this is described thus in the Qur'an:

Men, We have created you from a male and a female (Adam and Eve), and made you into nations and tribes,

that you might get to know one another. The noblest of you in God's sight is he who is most righteous. God is all-knowing and wise. (Al-Hujrat 49:13)

THE POOR AND BANKRUPT:

At one of the occasions the Prophet asked his companions, "who is the insolvent" (bankrupt). They said it is the one who may be penniless. To which the Prophet (peace be upon him) said which means that "The insolvent is that one who used to do lots of charities and good deeds in his lifetime - but at the same time he hurts this or harms that, and usurps the belongings of others, and lies or speaks about others, slanders them in their absence. On the judgment day, the rewards for his good deeds would be distributed among those whom he have hurt or harmed or took their belongings or talked or lied about them, until there is nothing or no good deed left for him from those rewards, and he still owes them. Then from whatever bad deeds they did will be deducted for the balance, and added onto the account of this person and then he will be thrown in fire (Hell)."

Now if we think about it who really could be more unfortunate than these bankrupt people who would lose all their good deeds and the rewards thereof, and then finds nothing left for themselves, except fire or hell, because of those wrong doings they did, and slander they made to others!

On another occasion! one of the companions asked the Prophet if people are thrown in hell just because of their sayings. The Prophet was sitting easily. When he heard this question he sat upright and told the enquirer angrily: which means, "you should know that people would be pulled by their tongues and thrown in the fire because of what had they used to say." (The liars, the cheaters, the one who speak about others in their absence or on their back, the slanderers etc.)

ALLAH IS FORGIVING AND MERCIFUL:

This verse is mentioned in many places in the Quràn. All believers believe in it whole-heartedly. But some times these gracious attributes of Allah are misunderstood and misused by some of the believers. They would not do what they were asked to do, like performing their obligatory rituals and duties, or they would do things they were forbidden to do, - and then murmur these verses. For sure Allah is forgiving and merciful, but that does not mean to take advantage of those attributes and character and we do not redeem it with our own endeavors to do our part of the obligations and not disobey His orders and commands. In another verse in the Quràn Allah promises to forgive whomever He wishes except those who believe in another deity or associate any partner to Him (polytheism).

We should understand the forgiving and merciful character carefully so as to avoid His wrath, also in a saying of the Prophet which means; "Allah does not blame from my people the ones who forgot or did inadvertent mistakes."

If we make unintentional mistake, or forgot to perform or observe a required ritual, due to forget-fullness or un-intentional mistakes, Allah is forgiving. Also if we did any wrong-doing we ask for His forgiveness, He will forgive. But if we continue wrong doings and insists on disobeying, then we should also remember that among His other tributes He is also severe or stern punisher. Let us give a very good example to understand and appreciate these attributes and characters and how we should reciprocate and thank Allah for His forgiveness and mercy.

One night Prophet's wife, Aysha Umm-Al Momineen, watched him praying nawafil or voluntary prayers for a long time, while standing up most part of the night, and his legs and feet become swollen. When he finished his worship, she said to him O Prophet of Allah why do you pray so much, didn't Allah promised to forgive you all your past or future days". The Prophet replied - which means "shouldn't I be a thankful (grateful) servant?" See, even though he is the Prophet of Islam *Mohammad* (peace be upon him), would not let opportunity passes without being a dutiful and grateful servant. He does perform and offers all the required obligations and duties, and in addition exerts all he can to do more and more to receive not only the forgiveness which he was already been promised for, but to attain the highest place in the sight of Allah and recieves his Blessings.

And so, Allah is Forgiving, but only to those whose mistakes or wrongdoings were un-intentional, and to those who would ask forgiveness, and do not insist or persist on doing the sin again and again. Also, God will not forgive those who associate any one or anything with him.

ANY MIDDLE MAN BETWEEN GOD & HUMAN BEINGS?!

There is no monasticism in Islam. People have to work and earn their living, helping themselves, their families and the others, and not sit in a secluded place, doing nothing except praying all their life. The people who can and do help others are better and nearer to God. People who keep themselves away from others and think or considers themselves above their fellow humans and that they are nearer to God are not acceptable or approved in Islam.

Also there is no in between the humans and their Lord. There is no middle person or agent between us and God. We should not go to some one else believing that he is authorized to ask God for help on our behalf or forgive our sins on His behalf. No one should claim to be the go between God and His creatures the humans. God did not delegate His authority to anyone to bestow His blessings and or to forgive or punishes anyone on His behalf.

When any one is in a dire need of help he asks God without even thinking. This motion comes instinctively, and God does help. And the help is swift, unless it is time - to go! But as human beings we all are allowed and encouraged to ask for God's help for our fellow human beings when they are in trouble. Like when someone we love is sick, we pray to God and ask Him for the well being and early recovery of our loved one. When an innocent person is wrongly and unjustly thrown in prison, we should pray to God and ask help for His release and acquittal. We should pray for the success of good ventures started by our fellow people. We all are his creatures and when we ask for God's help or forgiveness, we should rest assure of His kindness and acceptance of our prayers, without the need for a middleman or third person.

ADULT HOOD AND ITS RESPONSIBILITIES:

According to the Islamic teachings and information there in the Qur'an and the sayings of Prophet *Mohammad* (Peace be upon him), all mankind are passers by or travelers in this world. The travel date starts from the day we are born. We are welcomed pampered and fed and taken care of until we become old enough to know the surroundings and the people around us. We start walking and talking. We then are sent to school for education and learning, so that we may be able to handle our every day life properly when we became adults. "Adult hood" is the fine word where we start our life, knowing the good and the bad and differentiating between these two characters in our life, and be able to choose, decide and act on our own.

Adult hood, which varies between people, is the line or the beginning of where we accept the responsibilities of our activities and the resulting outcome, and the duties and delegations imposed on us. Adult hood is when people became mature enough to say yes or no to the things they see and understand as good or bad. From here starts the real account of what we will be doing throughout the rest of our life in this world. The complete activities of what we say or do will be accounted for. This is why we teach our children during their childhood every thing we know which could help them in their life-time, and before they attain their adulthood. What we teach them or whatever they see we are doing will be implanted and instilled in their mind and they may follow it after wards through-out their life, or they may not follow according to their nature, and the influences they may have around them. People are influenced by their parents, family members, friends neighbors, school and the society they live in, and most importantly by their spouse or the loved ones. Now-a-days they are also greatly influenced by the media, and what they read and see in the net or the TV channels, and most of which are wrong and bad influence.

Good people help others. This is why parents have the obligation to teach their children all the good manners and behaviors. They should teach and train them to be a good person. The children should learn to speak the truth and be honest. They should be admonished when they do wrong and should be rewarded by kind words and deeds when they do good. They should be trained to obey and fol-low the good deeds of their parents, guardians and teachers, so as to become useful members of their societies when they become adults and grow old. They should be shown how to worship God. They should be trained, and obtain the habits or accustomed to perform their obligations and duties since childhood. When people are taught and trained in their childhood the good manners or behavior they learn and attain will not go astray when confronted later on with any situation in their life. Because learning in childhood or at young age is imprinted and instilled in the brain or mind like the engraving on the stone, it stays in memory for ever.

In Islam when a person becomes adult he/she assumes the responsi-bility formally, for all the obligatory rituals and other responsibilities in life. They are from now on accountable for all their deeds, themselves. This is why it is very important for the parents, guardians and teachers to teach and instill good behavior, and the religious duties and respon-sibilities in young children so as to be able to assume good behaviors when they become young adults. Adult-hood is the age when a person feels the changes in his body. It is where a boy feels that he is becoming a man and the girl would know that she is becoming a woman.

DRESS CODE:

Dresses are made and worn according to the culture and habit of each society and where they live. They became used to it according to their needs and requirements, and also the materials which is available to them. It is also made according to the weather and environment requirements in their part of the world. It is different in the Sahara hot weather then the dress worn in the cold places of Siberia or the Northern cold areas. The most important function of the dress or the clothes is to protect the body from heat or cold and other environmental and weather effects.

Some dresses are liked, worn and became popular every-where. And some are but only for local or regional areas, and it is not liked or welcomed anywhere else. It is created and imposed on its societies by their own "haute couture"

Islam encourages its followers to be well dressed in a nice looking and clean attire, especially when going to pray and worship in the mosque. And there is no restrictions for Muslims to wear any dress which will make them look good, presentable and respected in any society they may live in.

In Islam it is required to cover the most important parts of the body - between the chest and the knees for men, and for women it should cover all their body. This is in conformity with the natural instincts and desires of human, as essentially the dress makes the distinction between human and the beasts.

There are some restrictions in the dress code for men. They should not spend extravagantly on their clothes and should not wear dresses made out of Silk material, or dress so long that it sweeps the floor behind, and also ornaments made out of Gold. These are prohibited for men, but are permitted for women. Men should not wear women's clothes or looks like women, and vice-versa, women should not dress or look like men. Women should not wear dresses which are explicit, transparent, tight and or short dress which shows and expose them and their body structure clearly. Islam insists on proper and respectable dress for men and women in their societies, to avoid the beastly looks and the allurement and desire.

CLEANLINESS:

"Neatness (or cleanliness) is part of the faith." This is a meaning of a saying of the Prophet of Islam (peace be upon him), emphasizing clearly on this subject. Islam urges strictly on its believers to adhere to the good custom of neatness and cleanliness. They should be clean not only in their outlook, but clean inside as well. They cannot offer their five times of prayers without being clean with ablution and have clean clothes. For performing Omra or Hajj and before wearing the Ehram for these rituals a Muslim should also have the ceremonial shower called he Ghosal.

When they go to lavatory, and after they have finished they should clean themselves very well with water (no dry cleaning or paper cleaning only). Then they should do the small ablution and wear nice and clean clothes before going for prayers to the mosques. There should be no filth or dirt or any bad stains clinging on their clothes. They should always keep their fingernails trimmed and clean. They should shave or remove clean their armpit and between the legs of their bushy hair, and keep it clean. Islam emphasizes a lot on cleanliness. The house should be clean, the eating and drinking utensils should be clean. The food they eat should be of clean material. No prohibited ingredients, like pork, swine lard or liquor in it.

The mouth should be clean and the breath should be nice and fresh, not smelly or staunchly. The Prophet of Islam *Mohammad* (peace be upon him) used to brush his teeth with Miswak, a small peace of branch of Arak tree, which is found in Arabia. It has the characteristic property of cleaning the tooth, healing and strengthening the gums. And he advise and encourages his companions and followers to use the Miswak for its good features.

ABLUTION OR (RITUAL CLEANING):

Before going to mosques for prayers Muslims should clean themselves and wear neat cloths. And for this reason there is a uniform way of cleanliness and it is called Wodou or ablution. There are two parts in ablution; one is the normal ablution Muslims should do before the prayers they offer. It is called the Wadou. And the other one is the Grand ablution, where in they have to wash themselves all over from the top of their heads until the bottom of their feet. It is called Ghosul:

WODOU'A:

If a Muslim did go to toilet for any of his nature's call, or releases gasses from his behind, then he becomes unclean. And so he should do the small ablution before he offers his prayers. Otherwise his prayers are unaccepted and are not counted It becomes null and void in the present terms. The way wodou'a is done is as follows:-

Wash and clean both hands thoroughly, first the right hand and then the left.

Wash and gargle mouth

Wash and rinse nose

Wash face all over 3 times

Wash right hand up to elbow 3 times and so the left hand and elbow.

Then pass the wet hands from the forehead until the end of the neck once. Wash the right foot first until the ankle and then the left foot, same way, thoroughly. And this is how the small ablution or Wodou, is done.

MAJOR RITUAL TO REMOVE IMPURITY (GHOSUL):

This ritual is done on and above the ablution. It is required to be done by both the man and the wife after sexual relation, ejaculation in dreams etc. It is also required for women to clean themselves after the menstrual period is completely finished.

After washing and cleaning their organs, the Muslim should do the ablution. The ritual of Ghosul to removes impurity. It is done by washing the head first then the right side of the body with water and then the left side. This way the whole body and curves are cleaned and purified with clean water. It is like having shower where all the body from top to toe is cleaned, after making the intention for Ghosul in one's mind.

WHAT IS TAYAMOM:

In certain instances a person may not be able to use water for cleanliness and ablution to offer the prayers. These situations are:

1. When there is no water available, like in the desert and barren land or away from dwelling or living places.

2. Water is available but may not be used, and may be harmful because of health hazard, like an injury and wounds.

3. Severe cold or sickness where a person may not be able to use water. These are some situations beyond our control. So, what should we do:

Like mentioned before in this book Islam does not force unto its followers or members things they cannot sustain or do. It takes the human capability into consideration. It made its rules lenient where and when required and according to real necessity. So in the above mentioned situation it has made an alternative for the small or the grand ablution. It is called the Tayamom.

How to do the Tayamom?:

It is done by hitting - gently - with the palm of both hands on the ground or any object where small dust may rise, and then slightly touch with both hands the forehead and the face, and then with each Palm of your hand wipe on the back of the other hand. We always use our right hand first, so in this case with the left palm we wipe the back of the right hand and then with the right palm wipe the back of the left hand slightly. It is simply a sign or a symbol of doing the ritual of ablution and purification. It is not necessarily to wipe the face or smear the hands with sand or dust to look sandy or dusty. It is done lightly, to offer the prayer which is due at that time, and should be done before each prayer time. And only for the time and period where no water is available - and or for the duration that a person cannot use the water for any reason.

At the time of the Prophet (peace be upon him) a person who had a head injury - had a wet dream in his sleep. His relatives and friends instead of purifying him with this ceremonial Tayamom, washed him and his head. He later died because of the infection caused or created by having water on his head injury. And when the Prophet knew and heard of this incident he was annoyd, and he told the relatives or friends of the deceased, "you killed your friend".

They should have used the tayamom method to avoid putting water on his injuries, which may have caused his death.

CHAPTER
16

CREATION OF MAN OR HUMAN

CREATION OF MAN OR HUMAN

God has created and molded Adam by Himself and blew His soul or spirit into him. And so humans are the most honoured of God's creatures. Because God intended humans to be His Caliph or successors in this world. They will be the successors by building in it and make it habitable, and worship God in it.

*(And I have created human and jinn (spirit) but to worship Me.){ 51:56}

They are to rule all other creatures because God have bestowed on human the mind. This mind is not bestowed on any other creatures in this world. It is not just an organ, which is the brain, but it is a think tank. It is the mind which enables human to think and visualize. It can interpret interpolate and summarize, and compare, by which it can come to a required conclusion. It can build and destroy. - It can calculate and computerize. It can learn and teach, understands and memorizes.

It can do by the power invested on it, thousands of operations by listening, visualize, compare and deciding, which no other being or creature in this world can do. Through this mind humans have the ability to listen, speak and talk. And through this mind they have the ability to differentiate and choose between the good and the bad, and between different objects and beliefs. When God announced His intentions to create man the Angels said: why create man who will bring destruction to the earth, while we are here to worship and obey you.

God told them that man will know all the names which He taught him, and they do not know it. So human beings with this mind know more than any other creatures and beings, and have the ability and power of decision making - which no other creatures have.

*[To understand this verse in its proper meanings, we know that all what we do as good deeds in this world will come under the word worship. God did not ask humans to sit all day long in the mosque or temple in a solitary place confining our self for the worship rituals only. Helping other humans in the name of God is also considered as worshiping.]

HIS TEACHING AND LEARNING:

The most important factor for the man is to learn and understand, and then he can choose and decide. Because without learning humans will live and act like animals.

And to teach humans and show them the right path and differentiate between right or wrong God sent His prophets and messengers to teach among them. They are sent among their own people to show and enlighten them.

Then it is up to them to decide, to deny or to accept. The messengers will also warn and caution them from doing wrong or bad deeds and tell them the consequence of their wrong decisions and bad deeds, which is depression, disappointment and shame in this world, and punishment in hell in the next world or next life after.

Also they will urge and encourage them to do the right and good deeds and tell them about the rewards or bounty they will expect and receive in reward of their good deeds and sayings - which will be happiness and blessings of God in this world, and the best life in heavens or paradise in the life after.

As a divine religion Islam also came to show us the right path which will lead humans into happiness and tranquility. It is a matter of fact religion which considers the human nature, and patronizes the good side of it, and discourages the bad side and stops it. It also defines clearly what are the good or the bad deeds.

Because it is the final divine revelations, Islam did not leave things for our imagination only. It clearly spells the things which its followers are supposed to do, and those that they should not do. It urges and encourages them on what to do, which is all the good things. And prohibits or forbids them from doing the things which are not supposed to be done, the evil and the bad deeds. And according to the teachings of Islam all good deeds are part of worshipping of Allah.

CHAPTER 17

SATAN (SHAITAN)

WHAT IS SHAITAN?:

Why people say or do bad or evil things? Who encourages or seduce them to do so? Why do they do all the bad things even though they know it is bad and they have a mind that can differentiate and distinguish between good and bad ?!

The people in this world are in a tug of war. This war is between the evil and the good. Unfortunately some people are more aligned or attracted with the bad or evil deeds. This is due to their own selfish nature which commands or urges its owner for the bad things. Faith or religions helps humans in fighting this selfishness to win the war against evils or bad deeds.

Nothing in this world can contain and stop people from doing evil deeds, except their faith or religion which they may believe in. There are the Ten Commandments which people should be adhering to. But when people's belief in their own religion and faith is weak and subsiding, then they do not adhere to these or any other teachings.

Why do people reach such a state of arrogance and self confidence that they forget who created them. And such people or persons may become the tyrants, atheists, and criminals who would harm their own family, relatives and society.

People in this state of freedom from faith and religion do not see the bad things as bad. And this is why they kill each other, dehumanizes, rob, and destroy and torture each other - because they do not believe in good or bad, and most important they do not even believe in God while doing their evil deeds.

They fight to kill others because they hate the others. They are afraid if they do not kill others- others will kill them. It is a cycle of self destruction which is initiated by some evil force and it is known as satanic force.

Satan or Iblis is the great Devil. When Allah (God) created ADAM, the father of humanity, by himself and then blew life into him. He then asked the angels to prostrate in front of Adam in respect as he was created by God Himself.

All the Angels did bow to this command except Ibliss or satan. This situation is described in the Holy Qur'an thus:

Your Lord said to the angels: 'I am creating human from clay. When I have (finished) making him and breathed of My spirit into him, kneel down and prostrate yourselves before him.'

The angels all prostrated themselves except satan (ibliss), who was too proud (arrogant), for he was an unbeliever.*

(Allah) said, O Iblees 'what prevented you from prostrating to him whom My own hands have made, Are you too proud, or do you think you are higher (than the human)

(Ibliees- satan) said: ' I am better than him. You created me from fire, and created him from clay.'

(Allah) said Get out of here as you are accursed' And verily, 'My curse shall remain on you until the Day of Reckoning.'

He (Iblees) said My Lord 'Reprieve me, till the Day of Resurrection.' (Allah) said: 'Reprieved you shall be till the Appointed Day.' (iblees) said 'I swear by Your glory,' 'that I will seduce (or mislead) them all, Except your faithful slaves amongst them' (Allah) said The truth is such and the truth I speak, That I shall fill Hell with your kind (offsprings) and with those of (humans) who follow you all together, (Saad 38: 71-84)

God has given reprieve to Satan/ Ibliss and granted him the time until the day of Judgment (or the end of this world),. And during that time he will try to seduce and lead astray the humans. He would make bad things look good and liked in the eyes and minds of people who would follow him. Thus his followers would bring on themselves the wrath of Allah, and bring on others the misery and problems.

The most devastating influence of the Satan (Shaitan) who adamantly challenged the will of God, is his promise to have the humans go astray and make them far from being good. Thus he does all he can to influence people badly through his ways and means of temptations, seducement or luring to make all bad deeds look nice and enjoyable in the eyes of the ones who are diverted from the right path and go astray, and become, killers seducers, rapists, loan sharks, etc etc.

Basically the wrong doers are people who are not close to the teachings of their religion. Because divine religions teach and advises people to do good, and restrains them from doing bad deeds.

Those wrong or evildoers, are people with no sense of goodness in them, and they may not have been taught and brought up in a good atmosphere. They are followers of satan. And some of these people becomes violent and could not be managed or accepted in a society. These are the unfortunate ones who did not take any chance or opportunity in their life for repentance, and died in-vain.

There are others who may have gone wrong or astray in some part of their life, but then relented and came back to their senses, and good nature and teachings.

They are the lucky ones, who repented and tried to straighten what wrong, they did and thus saved themselves in this world and the world thereafter. Allah has promised a good reward and a high place in heavens to those who repented and ask forgiveness, and will change their wrong doings into good deeds through his blessings. because they have caused a great disappointment, frustration and letdown to satan and his disciples.

For the believers of Faith and religions there is no choice but to fight all these problems, and fight the evils of Satan (Iblees). God has given humans the mind to think and the eyes to see what is right and what is wrong, and then follow the best. He also gave them the choice to accept what is better for themselves, which are the right things to do, and to refuse what they know is wrong. This tug of war between good and bad will continue for ever until the end of this world.

CHAPTER
18

GOOD DEEDS

GOOD DEEDS:

After passing this stage of belief, then every thing else would become easier to do and perform without reluctance. These are the things we have to do and perform in our lifetime here. Also there are things we should not do. What ever we say or do, good or bad, in this life will have an effect or impact on us or on the ones we did it to in this life and also in the life hereafter. Those are the Good and the Bad deeds. Islam aids and encourages its followers to do good deeds and say goods things and at the same time it abhors and discourages its followers from doing bad or evil deeds or sayings. Here are some of the Good deeds and some of the bad deeds:

WHAT ARE THE GOOD DEEDS:

These could be described in two ways:

(a)   Personal deeds which gives us the solace that we did perform all that we were supposed to do for our selves, like offering Prayers on time, fasting and doing other religious rituals. Besides the compulsory duties, we should offer voluntary prayers and rituals beyond the call of duty to achieve the blessings of God. We should not disobey God and should avoid doing bad deeds - no lies, no killings, no womanizing, no alcohol drinks or intoxicants, should not eat pork, do not eat orphans money or inheritance, no theft, do not in indulge in usury or loan sharking etc. These good deeds we do for our selves, and God almighty will rewards us generously for whatever good we do.

(b)   And the other good deeds we should do is for others, and it will bring us more and abundantly of God's favours. Those deeds are the ones we do to help others. And when we help others in this world we are actually helping ourselves too in this world and the other world of thereafter.

VOLUNTARY WORSHIP AND PRAYERS:

Good deeds in Islam: Allah urges the believers to do good deeds during their life time. He promised to give them ample rewards for whatever good deeds they make. These deeds are divided into two separate entities. One is to make the good deeds for personal benefit like the offering of volunteer prayers and worshipping to Allah.

The second deed is to do it to fellow human beings to help them in their needs and alleviate some of their hardships and misery. Like giving of charities, building mosques, hospitals, orphange, old people's home's and learning centers etc. In the first way or system the deeds are between the person and God, and in the second way they are between the person and other human beings. These charitable deeds benefits the receiver and also the giver - He gets the self satisfaction and solace that he was able to worship God, and was also able to help people in this world. And since he have done those charitable works or deeds in the name of Allah (God), and not for show-off or (attracting attention to himself), he is promised lots of rewards in the life after death. And the receiver of the charity is also satisfied that his needs are met.

Besides if you have a big wealth and did not spent it in good deeds - it will all be left here. A person cannot take anything with him except his deeds - Good or bad and that will make a big difference in the other life after resurrection, on the judgment day.

The first form of good deeds is between the person and God. It is the worship and prayers he offers to please Allah and obtain his blessings. These worships are in the form of offering voluntary prayers. These voluntary prayers are above and beside the compulsory prayers. It is also offered in times other than the assigned times of compulsory prayers.

1. These prayers are called the Nawafils prayers. For instance - there is the Doha prayers which is performed after sun rise and there are prayers which are offered late at night, wich is called Tahajjud.

2. In the voluntary worship is doing the fasting, like on Mondays and Thursdays, or the six days in the month of shawal after fasting the month of Ramadan, 9th, and 10th day of Moharram, and also the 9th of Dhul Hajj for the people who are not in Arafat performing the Hajj.

3. Also doing the Omra or small pilgrimage, especially during the month of Ramadan, comes in the voluntary worship.

4. Giving charity to the poor on and above the Zakat is also a voluntary prayer.

Voluntary worship and prayers are done seeking the pleasure of God and His blessings and also asking God for help during hard ship and bad time. And if it is not done, it does not count as sin or misdeed and does not constitute any offence. These are voluntary rituals and people are urged and encouraged to do it for their own good and benefit, and to receive more blessings and rewards.

And the second form of voluntary worship and good deeds are the deeds between a person and his fellow human beings which includes helping people financially, physically and otherwise especially the needy ones, and it is called charity. It is suggested that the charity begins at home. For instance people should help their relatives who are indeed in need, then extend it to others wherever it can be afforded and offered.

Sadaqat (Charities):

Poverty is a social evil. It could generate lots of problems in a society-people lose dignity under the pressure of poverty - Some people would take advantage of these poor and may force them to do things they would not do otherwise.

Islam recognizes these short comings of poverty, and force-fully tries to cure the illnesses and short comings of poverty. It understands that the living circumstances are different among different sect of people. Some people have more then the others - It is because of so many, and various reasons.

Charities are in many forms: you should relieve the ones who are in dire need of financial or physical help- Be lenient on the ones who have borrowed from you and are not able to pay back in time. Even removing obstacle from the pathways to make it safe for the passers-by is also a form of charity. Those good deeds we did or do for others are called charities.

Charities means we help the needy and helpless, saving some ones life by giving immediate help - opening charitable hospitals, Schools orphanage, residence for the elders, etc. etc.

The Prophet tells us that a person went to heaven because he saw a thirsty dog and used his shoe to fill it with water he drew from a well to help the dog drink and quenched his thirst. That also was a charity.

Whatever good we may do in this life is accumulated and compensated to us, and will help us attain higher places in heaven.

Generally charities should not be more then ? (one third) of a person's assets or funds, and one third also is too much, as mentioned by the Prophet. If some one gives all what he have in charities, and leaves nothing for himself and his relatives or the heirs and leaves them poor, then the purpose of the charity is misunderstood and its purpose is defeated. Islam does not allow doing good to some while hurting others. It does not urges you to give all what you have and leave nothing for your selves and your immediate relatives and family, or the probable heirs.

ISLAM ABHORS SELFISH-NESS:

A saying of the Prophet *Mohammad* (peace is upon him) which means that no body is a believer until he likes for his brothers what he loves for himself. Literally it means that Muslims should not be selfish, and encouraging them to be selfless and should consider the benefits which they may like for themselves, they should like it for others too. They should let good things happen to others as well as to themselves, and help or assist in that.

Charities are not necessarily the financial aspect, especially when we do not have the means. But an attempt to help even through others constitutes a charity, and bring rewards for the one who attempted and pursued to help through others, besides the ones who actually paid for or did the help. Both will receive big rewards.

The Prophet says, which means: who ever relieves his brother's suffering (grief) in this world, God will relieve him from a suffering (grief) on the Day of Judgment.

Some Charities are a temporary relief, like giving poor passer by some money, food or drink to relieve their urgent need - now.

And some charities are for a long standing relief. It is like forgiving some or all of your debt on some one who is incapable of paying his debt back because of unforeseen circumstances, establishing fund for charitable purpose described before.

Islam emphasizes on all charity works and informs us that whatever charities we are giving in this world in the name of Allah it is accumulated for us with all our good deeds in the life hereafter and will bring substantial rewards to us from Allah after we die. Giving a half piece of date (or half a sandwich for that matter) which a person may only have at the time, to a needy poor follow will get that person a big reward and save him from hell.

YOU OWE ME ONE!!!:

There is an important aspect of charity or any good deed people may make in the name of Allah to obtain higher and plenty of rewards from Him. Make these good deeds without bragging about it to each and everyone - other wise it will defeat the purpose of the these good deeds - and you will receive only what you are asking for - the admiration of some people - and the wrath of God - who does not like that his poor subjects be defamed by this unnecessary bragging.

Also you do not give some one a charity and then whenever you see him you say "you owe me one!!!" This way he will owe you nothing. You are trying to hurt his sense of pride and feelings, which Islam does not allow or encourage. You never know when you may need him or any one else -later on, and the life hereafter.

WHAT ARE THE REWARDS:

Whatever good deeds, or however small it might be will fetch a generous reward from Allah. The Prophet says which means: "Whoever relieved a suffering or a grief for a brother in this world Allah will relieve a big grief or suffering from him in the Day of Judgment". This is one way of getting a reward.

The other ways are alleviating or reducing some or all of the punishments and being forgiven, and the time left in hell will be reduced, and sent to heaven earlier. (serving less time for good behaviour). And promotion to a higher place in heavens or paradise, because of these charities and good deeds.

So even though we think we did a favour to others in this life, as a matter of fact we are doing our selves more favour. and the benefit is for all. So it would be silly not to avail the opportunities of doing good while we are alive. And there are so many ways to do good in this short life.

God is kind and Merciful and Just - God dislikes injustice or oppression. He deals with justice and compassion to all humans. He made the punishment of our wrong doings just according to the size or measure of our bad deeds.

But for the rewards and bounties, there is no limit - it becomes according to His will and wishes. If some one did a good deed because he had to do it, it is different from the one who wished to do it and most willingly did it. It is a big difference, and so the rewards also becomes as significant as his desire to do it.

As a general rule, we are told that good deeds are rewarded ten times, and would increase up to seven hundred times of its size and, again it may go to unlimited according to the blessings of Allah

And also the reward comes according to the desire of the one who did it. Did he do it especially to please Allah and seeking His bless-ings or did he do it for different purpose and desires like showing off! Like when some one who gives a charity and he wants every one to know about it and say "what a big philanthropist he is". Then he gets nothing in the next life because he already got his reward here and the people said - "What a great philanthropist he is" and this was his rewards which he desired to get from the people - and he got it. His desire was not to seek the blessings of Allah alone.

We mentioned about the good deeds. Now here are some of the bad deeds, which we are strongly urged to avoid, mentioned in the next chapter.

CHAPTER 19

BAD AND EVIL DEEDS

NOT BELIEVING IN THE ONENESS OF GOD:

The worst thing for anyone to happen is to become aloof and ignores the first and most important belief of the existence. It is the belief in God, and in His oneness. And the other worst act some people would do is to enjoin any or some one or something along with God. The first category are the atheist, and the second types are the polytheists.

These kind of people are the most unfortunate ones in the life after death. Because in their arrogance and blind ignorance, and their insisting refusal of this belief, they have called the wrath of Allah upon them selves.

They live in this world without the self conscious and inner comfort solace, and they may do whatever they can, but would not expect any remuneration or compensations which otherwise the believers would expect to get in the life after.

They are described as people living in this world as cattle's live. They live aimlessly, and without sense of responsibility and understanding. They are the people whom God has clearly warned that He will not forgive.

WHAT ARE THE BAD OR EVIL DEEDS?!

At an occasion when asked what are the most evil deeds, the Prophet said which means, "polytheism, the disobedience of parents and saying of false testimony". There are many other grave sins and bad deeds which are mentioned and cautioned against by the Prophet of Islam at different occasions.

These grave sins and evil deeds derives shame and problems in this life and a greater retribution and punishment in the life after a person dies. Some of these are mentioned as follows:

Polytheism: is joining or associating any one or anything with God or believing in the power of any one else to be as equal to God's.

This could be in the form of making statues, idols and placing them at home or in other places, and worshipping it in anyway or form, or asking it for any help whatever it might be, or believing in it or in any person or anything, that they may have the power or the characteristics like God's.

The biggest of the evils is associating any one with God, or believing in some one as relating to God, or in another deity or partner for Him. Believing in any form of polytheism is forbidden in Islam and it is considered the greatest sin. God says in Holy Qur'an,"

God will not forgive who ever makes a company (or associates partners) for him, but he may forgive for other things to whom ever He wishes.

DISOBEDIENCE OF PARENTS:

Disobedience of parents is a grave sin In Islam. The parents should have great love, respect and obedience. Believers are strongly urged to respect and obey their parents and favour them, especially when they are old. If they do not have any personal income, we are obliged to provide them with all what they need (naturally, within our own means) house them, feed them and take good care of them. They are to be dealt with care and respect even if both or either one of them is not a true believer.

When our parents are happy with us, then we expect the blessings of Allah onto ourselves and our family and children. And if they are not happy, because of mistreatment by us, then we may expect the wrath of Allah, unless they became happy and forgive us for any disregard, disobedience or disrespect which we may have done.

It is generally known that the people who mistreated their parents, may themselves be treated as such or worse by their own children when they attain old age. So, why don't we avoid this lousy situation, by taking good care of our parents while we can.! In the Qur'an, it is mentioned in many places about how the parents should be treated or taken care of:

"And your Lord has decreed that you worship none but Him, and be kind unto your parents when either or both of them attain old age while they are with you (in your lift-time), say not to them a word of disrespect and do not rebuke them, address them (speak with them) in terms of honour. (17:23)

And lower unto them the wings of submission and humility through mercy (kindness) and say 'My Lord bestow on them (Your) merey as they did bring me up when I was young'. (17:23)

FALSE TESTIMONY:

Islam teaches us to be truthful in our dealings and it abhors lies and liars. Especially when we are required to testify. No one should give false testimony. Because this abuse of the trust, may hurt the right causes with false testimony. And it may hurt not just a single person, but it will hurt all the ones around him, or who may have dependence on him. False testimony will hurt the society on the whole. Judgments are based on the testimony, a false testimony will make the right to a wrong and the wrong is made right. And it is deceiving some people of their rights, and making for others what does not belong to them. So it is considered a big sin. Also, when required to give testimony, Muslims should not abstain from saying the truth because if we abstain from saying the truth it is again harmful to the ones who needed the right testimony to enhance their true cause, and obtain their right.

KILLING OR MURDER:

The first killing in human history is when (Abel) Habil was killed by his brother (Cain) Qabil for the love of their sister. These were the sons of Adam and eve the Father and Mother of humanity. Islam does not allow the unlawful killing of any human being. It does not even allow the unnecessary killings of animals. And severe punishments for the perpetrators, of the crime of killing is promised by Allah in the here after:

{ 4:93} **If a man kills a believer intentionally his recompense is Hell to abide therein (for ever): and the wrath and the curse of Allah are upon him and a dreadful penalty is prepared for him.**

{ 5:32} **On that account: We ordained for the Children of Israel that if anyone slew a person unless it be for murder or for spreading mischief in the land it would be as if he slew the whole people: and if anyone saved a life it would be as if he saved the life of the whole people. Then although there came to them Our apostles with clear Signs yet even after that many of them continued to commit excesses in the land.**

USURY - INTEREST - LOAN SHARKING:

This is one of the worst way people would treat each other or compensate with their societies they live in. And these dealings are unacceptable in Islam. The Interest or Usury system harms the society in its living. It makes the living hard at best, and God has promised worst punishment for the people dealing in usury and interest.

Among the punishment in this world, the depression occurring in the belongings and assets of both the borrowers who borrow because of dire needs and who have to pay the interest, and the lenders who gives the loan and takes interest. Even though the lenders may think their money or account is increasing because of the interest they are obtaining, but in reality and for unseen reasons it is dwindling at the same time through natural or other causes and calamities, and eventually lots of problems befalling them and their business and or financial entity before it finally collapses.

Besides the depression of his assets and belongings the loan shark or the lender also becomes a very unpopular person in society. And in time he becomes harsh, and he starts treating his borrowers with extreme harshness and inhumanity. And all will despises him.

At the same time the ones who took the loan will sink deeply in the mud of interests. Eventually they may have to sell their belongings and property only to survive the interest they or their heirs or inheritors have to pay. They will become the slave of this loan which is accumulating interest every day, and it becomes so big that eventually it cannot be paid. It is not a fair dealing, especially for the borrower who took the loan because of their urgent or dire needs.

Few recent examples of how interest or usury brings havoc to the economy of societies and harms it instead of bringing any prosperity to it.

One of the biggest and well known Airline in the 60's which used to fly around the world twice a day. One flight from the west flying towards the east, and the other is from east to west. This famous international air liner eventually succumbed and closed down, as it could not pay even the interest alone, to their lenders which accumulated into hundreds of Millions, even after the sales of its most impressive building it could not pay back, and declared bankruptcy and was gone, leaving thousands of its employees without jobs.

And so did few other airlines which grew up fast anded end up faster because of not being able to pay the interest on their loans, leaving the main amount of borrowing intact. Is it worth it that tens of thousands of people lose their jobs and investments in such a lucrative business, because of interest.!!?

In the same era a huge financier Bank which had deposits and savings for thousands of people, and had assets in the range of billions went bankrupt in one day. Next day thousands of people lost their jobs, and thousands lost their accumulated wealth and savings, which was in their savings account, and which they expected would increase through interest. But instead it was all lost, because of usury or interest.

A recent one is a conglomerate worth billions was closed down and become worthless the next day. Regardless of where these closures happened or are happening every day, around the world, the main culprit in all of those big losses is the interest or usury in whichever form or false name it might be, besides other ills like bad management.

Even countries and nations would and were paralyzed once in a while because of this problem. If it were not for the oil flowing with the blessing of Allah, many countries dealing in interest would have succumbed due to its economic failures which is partly run by money borrowed in interest.

This situation is in this world, and the bankruptcy following both the lenders and the borrowers. How about the there after, when the lender goes from this world and finds himself Bankrupts there also? It is not a nice feeling, isn't it?!

In Qur'an it is mentioned that those people dealing in interest will wake up in the day of Judgment and they find themselves like the one who is stumbling from craziness or insanity.

He walks like he is in a series of bumps and being hit by the devil.

So Islam deems usury or interest as a great evil and sin, and it rejects the dealings in it, in whatever form or name. And it is mentioned in the Qur'an:

[2: 257] THOSE THAT live on usury shall rise up before God like men whom satan has demented by his touch; for

they claim that trading is no different from usury. But God has permitted trading and made usury unlawful. He that has received an admonition from his Lord and mended his ways may keep his previous gains; God will be his judge. Those that turn back shall be the inmates of the Fire, wherein they shall abide forever. God has laid His curse on usury and blessed almsgiving with increase. God bears no love for the impious and the sinful. Those that have faith and do good works, attend to their prayers and render the alms levy, will be rewarded by their Lord and will have nothing to fear or to regret.

{2: 278} Believers, have fear of God and waive what is still due to you from usury, if your faith be true; or war shall be declared against you by God and His apostle. If you repent, you may retain your principal, suffering no loss and causing loss to none.

If your debtor be in straits, grant him a delay until he can discharge his debt; but if you waive the sum as alms it will be better for you, if you but knew it.

{2: 281} Fear the day when you shall all return to God; when every soul shall be requited according to its deserts. None shall be wronged.

ADULTERY OR FORNICATION:

We said in the beginning, Islam protects women and treat her with respect if she stays Pious and clean and do not indulge herself, or being lured by the men who may try to rob her of her respect and vanity in so many different names and vague slogans as women's lib or women's rights.

Adultery is not only forbidden in Islam; it is also forbidden in all beliefs and religions, and it is treated as a big sin and great offence.

Generally it is a sin which spreads all kinds of social, physical and human problems and diseases. It makes the people who indulged in it without dignity or respect. It spreads poverty and tear down the fabric of family and society.

At the time of Prophet *Mohammad* (peace be upon him) a young man came to him while he was in the mosque. And in front of the companions of the Prophet, who were there, he said to the Prophet that he came to embrace Islam (accepts Islam) but he had one condition to accept Islam; that because he is young and have a lot of energy and desire for women, he may be allowed to indulge in adultery (fornication).

Prophet *Mohammad's* companions became angry and agitated at this outburst of disrespect. But the Prophet "peace be upon him" did not get angry. He was smiling; He asked the young man to come closer to him, He put his hand on the young man's chest and asked him a direct question, which means "Do you accept this to happen to your mother."

The young man was taken aback, and he replied - no, he would not accept such a hideous thing to happen to his mother.

Then he was asked if he would accept or agree that some one would ask his Aunties for this purpose. The young man said - no he would not allow this to happen to his aunts. He was asked would he agree if it is done to his sisters. The young man really was aghast and did not agree for this also.

Prophet *Mohammad* (peace be upon him) then asked the young man, how come he agrees to do it to others and does not agree that it happens to his own family, and the women in his house hold.

The young man was ashamed and he promised the Prophet (peace be upon him) that he will never again do this sinful act or think about it, while embracing Islam.

This sinful act derives a lot of disgrace and shame in this world, beside all the ailments and diseases it can spread in the society, and harsh punishment later, in the next life.

DRINKING, DRUGS AND GAMBLING:

Intoxication and Gambling are two enjoined evil deeds - and it is mentioned in the Qur'an together, because of its interrelated vicious outcome. It is a very serious crimes against the family, loved ones and the society. Before the advent of Islam, people used to make liquor or wine, and some of the Prophets companions used to drink. The stoppage of this evil habit started coming gradually. In one occasion some people came to offer their prayers while they were tipsy or intoxicated and they would not perform their prayers rightly and recite the Qur'an properly. And the revelation came.

"Do not come near the prayers and you are intoxicated."

Later on came the all time renouncement of drinking along with other wrong and evil deeds like gambling and divination which are described as dirty or filthy works of Satan, and admonished Muslims not to do it.

{ 3:90} BELIEVERS, WINE and games of chance, idols and divining arrows, are abominations devised by satan. Avoid them, so that you may prosper.

{ 3:91} Satan seeks to stir up enmity and hatred among you by means of wine and gambling, and to keep you from the remembrance of God and from your prayers. Will you not abstain from these?

These revelations made the drinks and Gambling Haraam or Unlawful. In Islam drinking intoxicants or any alcoholic drinks is considered the great evil, or the mother of sins. Because a person who is intoxicated looses his consideration for himself, the ones around him and even the ones with him. He may do anything nasty and wrong to anyone without any considerations. So is Gambling which creates hatred and animosity among people involved in it. Many a time people dealing in gambling became enemies of each other and lost their fortunes, assets and belongings, and became worthless persons and harmed their own families.

As for drugs, by using it a person harms himself mostly, and becomes an invalid member of the family, and society. It is therefore not permitted. Because in Islam a person should be a valuable and good person for himself, his family, and the society at large. Islam teaches that you should not even harm or hurt yourself, directly and or indirectly.

CHAPTER 20

LIFE AFTER DEATH

THE LIFE AFTER DEATH:

After coming into in this world each one of us will spend our life time and then all of us will be passing away. So in this world we are passers by, and not a single one will stay here for ever!. This world is a transit area for us on the way to another world of permanent life.

In our short or long life span according to the time we spent in this world, we should be doing what is best for us in this life and the life there after. Since we are in transit area, we might as well take advantage of the time we have here and do all the needful, and obtain all that is possible to help us in acquiring a better place and position in the next life, which is the life after death. We should take or obtain lots of gifts, as good deeds, with us, while we can, now.

People should believe in this coming life, the life after-death, and should be prepared for it. What are the preparations:- The first and most important of the preparations for the next life we will be going to is "The believe in Allah, God and Lord of everything, and believe in His Oneness. This is the main belief which would help us in the life after. If we do not believe in this main gist of beliefs, than how or whom we would ask for help, when we are going to need that help?!

WHAT KIND OF LIFE AFTER DEATH:

There are three kinds of people in the life of after death.:

1.   The believers, who believed in the oneness of God and in Mohammed (peace be upon him) as his messenger, who did good and tried to avoid bad saying deeds.

2.   Those believers who committed sins and did not perform their religious duties, and did not ask for forgiveness.

3.   The non-believers ~ atheists ~ Polytheists.

The first, and most fortunate ones are those who passed their life in this world believing in God and in His Oneness, and they observed and offered what was required of them of prayers and rituals, and good deeds.

They also avoided to do any wrong doings, or if they did, they may have asked forgiveness of their bad deeds. Their sins or bad deeds would be converted to a good ones when they asked forgiveness and felt ashamed or remorse for their mistakes and did not insist or persist on their wrong doings during their lifetime.

They may have offered many voluntary prayers, besides doing the compulsory ones, in its proper form. They may also did many good deeds in their life expecting its rewards not from the ones they did it for, but from God Almighty whose rewards are insurmountable. These are the lucky and fortunate people who would go to very high places in heaven after they receive their accountability book of their life by their right-hand. Because in the Day of Judgment people will receive their progress report, a book in which mentioned all what they did in their lifetime. Good or Bad. Accordingly, the people who are lucky and fortunate, and did lots of Good deeds will receive their book by their right hands.

"He that is given his book in his right hand shall have a lenient reckoning, and shall go back rejoicing to his people."

The second, type or kind of people are those who were just fortunate enough to pass the first test or condition of belief; and accepted it and believed in it. These people may have done bad deeds, or they did it too many times without remorse or asking for forgiveness, and they did not comply and perform their required duties and obligations of the compulsory prayers and rituals required of them. These people are less fortunate as they are punished, and have to suffer their punishment or part of it in hell.

Their deeds in their life time were totally bad. They are the killers, the liars, thieves and looters, bandits, harmful to their relatives and neighbors and the whole society they lived in. They were the extortionists, the rapists and so forth.

After paying their dues or serving their sentences, they will be freed from hell and are allocated a place in heaven and sent there to spend the rest of their life in Heaven. They are given the reduction of their sentences or pardon whole or partially by the blessings of Allah - because they believed in Allah and in His Oneness.

The third kind of people and most unfortunate ones are those who are destined to go to Hell and stay there forever. They are the non believers, the atheists, and the ones who believe in polytheism or in the associating of God with some one else. They are the most unfortunate ones, because they will stay in hell for "ever". "Forever" is a long time in life. It has no time limit. It is infinite or unaccountable. There is no end, when we say forever. Who would bring for themselves this worst situation except, the unfortunate and miserable ones.

And the unfortunate ones will receive their book by their left hand, or from their back. They were not the believers, and they were the adamant staunch refusals of the belief in Allah, and or they associated with him anyone else. Their place is destined in hell.

This scene is described in the holy Qur'an as such:

But he that is given his book behind his back shall call down destruction on himself and burn in the fire of Hell; for he lived without a care among his people" [84:13]

HOW PEOPLE ARE COMPENSATED FOR THEIR DEEDS:

Allah (God) is the Lord of each and every thing. All people in this world are His subjects. He bestows and allows the grade or ranks and positions so that our worldly affairs would function and work properly and every one becomes responsible for whatever his position and job derives or describes.

There are hundreds if not thousands of grades and positions from being on the top of the level like a King or President to the lowest rank of a soldier, and whatever comes in between. From the CEO or chairman of a corporation to its janitor. The head of a household to the last one who works.

Each and every one is responsible, and will be questioned about the well being or welfare of their subjects, workers and protégé, in the life after death.

There is a saying by Prophet *Mohammad* (peace be upon him) which means: "You all are guardians (custodians or keepers /supervisors), and every guardian is responsible (questionable) about his subjects or herd or flock. The man is guardian in his house and he is responsible for his wife and family. And the woman is responsible about her house and her family!" Thus every one of us has a responsibility about himself, his family his children and about his work and his job.

Everyone will be questioned about how he did his work, how he fared with the people he was entrusted with and about their welfare and well being. If fared well, then we are successful and will be granted good rewards and high position in heaven. But for those who neglected their responsibilities and did not do their job well, or did excessive wrong doing or were unjust with their subjects and workers - then there is no one to blame but oneself - who did not do their job fairly or at least tried to do it well.

The people who will fare badly and are among the most unfortunate in the life after death, are the tyrants, despotic, unjust and oppressors, who mercilessly killed and destroyed people without justice and mercy.

So when anyone thinks that because of his might and position in this world he can hurt people, he should think twice of what would happen to him after he dies, it will be hell. It is very serious and painful situation, and the wise would and should try to avoid going in there - in hell. In the holy Qur'an there is a word of caution, which means:

O believers, protect yourself and your family from fire (hell) the fuel of which is humans and rocks. It has strong Angels who do not disobey Allah and His commands, and verily they do what they are ordered to do.

(Most of us must have seen the boulders of fiery firy rocks blown up high or tumbling down on volcanic mountains- it does gives the readers an idea of what the Qur'an is talking about when describing the human and rocks as the fuel of hell.)

The people who suffered, and died at the hands of tyrants and despondent in this world, will receive the justice, solace and comfort in the life after death, and in the Judgment day in the form of large rewards and great compensations for the pain and agony they have received and suffered. The rewards would be much more and greater than their expectations. And that will make them so happy that they wish they had suffered more to receive more rewards.

But those tyrants who have committed those crimes and tyranies would wish that they were never born and have not done those evil deeds, and would not receive such a painful punishments.

WHAT TO TAKE OR EXPECT AFTER DEATH?:

The Prophet of Islam says which means that when a person dies he is cut off from this world, and his actions come to an end except for three things (which will continue to effect him even after his death, and which he leaves behind). Those are:

1.   **The continuous act of charity.**

2.   **The knowledge (or Book) which people will benefit from.**

3.   **And a dutiful child, who will pray for him.**

To understand this Saying or Hadith of the Profet we explain as follow:

1.   A persons own sayings and deeds in his lifetime will make the difference between the luxurious life and the blessings he is granted in Heavens or the wretched life and torture he receives in hell. Good deeds are beneficial, for the one's who are doing it and for the ones who are receiving it. Many things would come under good deeds; the least is clearing the way from obstacles which might hurt people. Giving charities, establishing charitable funds, opening training centers and schools, free hospitals, dispensaries, orphanages, old care center for the poor etc. All for free or just a nominal charges to continue the charity. Giving loans without interest, paying to release people from their misery, building mosques, etc. etc., are good deeds which would bring the blessings of Allah in this world, and the world after, where he attains a higher place in heaven.

Establishing any of these charitable acts through a foundation or continous funds will benefit the dead even after his death, and for a long time to come.

2.   A knowledge or a good book from which people may learn and benefit. We may give some charity to people, it is an instant favour which may finish with the dwindling or end of the charity. And the person may need the same help again and again from us or from others.

But if we teach this person how to earn his own livelihood - like teaching him a vocation or trade, this way we help him to be independent and he does not need the help from us or from others all the time. Besides he will be helpful to his own family and dependents. This kind of knowledge which we pass on to others and which helps them in their livelihood is also being considered as a knowledge we left for others to benefit themselves from. This act of goodness does help us also in our lives after leaving this world to the next life.

3.   A good and dutiful child (sons and daughters) who would pray and then ask Allah to grant pardon to their deceased Parents and would ask Allah to grant him a benefit and good place in heaven and bestow mercy on him. Also whatever good deeds his offspring does will add to our own good deeds and blessing, for our benefit, without shortage of the benefits they get from their good deeds.

AND WHERE TO GO AFTER DEATH?:

Simply put there are only two places to go after death. It is heaven or hell. The believers had will go to heavens. They will go there even after passing hell for sometime and has paid their dues of misdeeds they did in this world, and finally obtain the pardon and mercy of Allah, then they are taken to heaven. They will ask Allah during their life time for mercy, and Allah is the most merciful. He grants his pardon and mercy to whom ever he wishes and chooses.

The believers are sent and guided with blessings of God to heavens where they are greeted and welcomed. They will enter it with peace and solace. They will enjoy their comfortable and luxurious living in there for ever.

But what about the unbelievers, atheist or polytheists, they will be in real trouble. Because, for the first category which are the atheists; How they may plead now and from whom they may ask for help, or pardon or mercy? They did not even think or believe in the existence of God. Whom are they going to ask for pardon now? Because after death every one is cut off from this world and since they did not ask this pardon before death, how may they ask now? And whom they may ask? They have no one to turn to for any help! Miserable situation?!

As for the polytheists; they would be told to ask for help from the ones they associated with Allah, or from their deities or statues they made themselves and worshipped instead of bowing to Allah, who is the Greatest and Lord of everything. They will find that they have no one to help them either. Because there is no God except Allah. They will also be in bad situation!

These unfortunate ones of the second and third group who are the unbelievers, they would be herded towards hell where they would stay and suffer punishment for ever. Let us think about it. People in arrogance refuse to accept the right things. They are proud, they think they are smart and powerful. Until when, one stays powerful? Until what age? And then what? No power, no grace and no believe? They lose every thing.

What would happen to them if they believed in God and the oneness of God?! Here they are not the losers. They are the winners. They win themselves from being sent to hell for ever. This belief and the acceptance of the existence of Allah, and in His oneness should come well ahead of time before dying and not in the last moment of the death. Also, nobody knows when sudden death comes. It comes suddenly. So the opportunity for repentance and the chance to ask for pardon or mercy is suddenly missed or gone... for ever!

But when they adamantly defy this truth with their arrogance and false pride and pretense, which Satan have instilled in them - they become the losers, and losers for ever. The sensible and wise people should think before they die. Because after death there is no return back and no more arguing or asking for pardon or forgiving. In this world we have the opportunity to save ourselves from suffering after death.

Pharaon, the powerful king of Egypt and who proclaimed himself as a God, accepted this belief just before he was dying, drowning in the Sea, but it was too late for him, and it is described thus in the Qur'an:

10:90. And We took the children of Israel across the sea, and Fir'aun (Pharaoh) and his legion followed them in oppression and enmity, till when he was drowning, he said: "I believe that there is no God exists except the God in which the Children of Israel believe, and I am one of the Muslims (now)

10:91. Now (you believe) while you refused to believe before and you were one of the Mufsidûn (evil-doers and the corrupters)

10:92 So this day We shall deliver your (dead) body (out from the sea) that you may be a sign to those who come after you! And verily, many among mankind are heedless of Our Ayât (proofs, evidences, verses, lessons, signs, revelations, etc.). (10 : 90 - 91 - 92)

CHAPTER
21

END OF THE WORLD

END OF THE WORLD:

Our life in this world is short compared to the life after death, which becomes eternal - and no more death, as explained before in the earlier chapter The life on this planet we live on is also short compared with what is coming for us or where we are going to, after this worldly life.

Some day this world will come to an end. And that would be the judgment day. That is the day when all and every one will believe in the existence of Allah (God), and will believe in His making and the great power He does have. But alas, it will be too late for the nonbelievers then!

That is the judgment day when every one will be judged and awarded the final verdict. When will that be,? No one knows. But Prophet *Mohammed* (peace be upon him) told us about the signs and indications which will happen before the arrival of that day will come.

Among those important signs are the coming of (Gog and Magog) Yajjoj and Majooj. Those are the people who would come from the east and they will eat and drink and finish each and every thing eatable, or drinkable on their way.

Also, before the end of the world the tyranny and oppression will be rampant. People will make the right wrong and the wrong right, with the knowledge they have learnt and the power they may have attained.

All bad deeds or activities would be popular. Women will have no value, they will bare their clothes, and shameful activities of seduction and wrong doings will be the norm. There would be no solace, tranquility or peace of mind.

In this period of extreme chaos would arrive Jesus Christ, son of holy mother Mary (peace be upon them). He will descend from heavens on earth and he will rule the world with justice, and will restore peace and tranquility. In his short time there will be no injustice, and justice will prevail, every where.

THE RISING SUN FROM THE WEST:

The last and most important sign will be the rising of the sun from the west. It will rise until it becomes in the middle of the sky for a short while, and then reverses its course and staggers on its correct rotation towards the west. This would be the last sign of the advent of the day of Judgment. When this Solar anti movement happens, it will be the end of the believe time, and the closure of the gates of repentance and forgiveness. And from there on it would be waiting for the end. Until the day the horns would be blown and every thing would die from the unbearable shriek of the sound of the horns. And that would be the judgment day.

JUDGMENT DAY / DOOMS DAY:

It is the day when the horn will be blown, and it will be such aloud noise (may be, exceeding thousands of decibels!) that every living thing in this world will freeze to death because of the unbearable sound, and fright. Then things would be so frightening that pregnant women would drop or give birth instantly. People will be dazed and every living thing will die. It really will be hell breaking lose. And the mountains would be broken and it would fly as cotton buds, and the oceans would be ignited into fire balls.

Then the horn will be blown again, and the resurrection starts. No one knows how much time will be between the first and the second sound. Every one will rise up from where ever it was buried or blown. People will rise from their graves, or from where ever they may be. We should not be surprised how this is going to happen. Who created us from a small sperm and created large trees from small bean would re-create each and every one again. When God commands to anything to "Be", it will happen. It becomes, instantly! People will rise from the dead as they were from when or where ever they were. They will be without their clothes, fearsome looking. Umm Al momineen lady Ayesha, a wife of the prophet asked "O prophet of Allah, even the women will be seen like that, " The prophet answered which means "O Ayesha, that day would be so gruesome that no one cares about this matter."

Then all the people would be herded towards the "Gathering Ground." It will be so big a place, where each and every individual from the time of Adam and Eve until the day the whole things come to an end, will be gathered in it.

In the Gathering Ground all will be awaiting to see the account and the results of their life time. Because that will also be the judgment day! On judgment day there will be a fair trial and the proper judgment will be the out come for everyone. It will be either heavens or hell. God has given us humans the chance and choice to work and ask for His forgiveness and blessings - while we are still alive in this world. To be eligible for heaven one must have been obedient to God and His commandments, and be useful and helpful and kind to his fellow human beings. Tyrants, despots and killers and the disobedients would expect to be on the other side - which is hell.

WHAT ARE HEAVEN AND HELL:

For the life after death Allah has created two distinct places. Those are proper places for the people who deserve it according to the their beliefs, sayings and deeds. And these two places are Heavens and Hell.

HEAVENS (PARADISE):

It is the place which is being promised to all the believers in God, Allah. It is a place made for maximum comfort especially for the believers who did well, and also those who suffered a lot at the hands of tyrants and oppressors. The best description for heavens is what the

Prophet (peace be upon him) said that means, **"There are things in there that are never been seen and never been heard of, and did not come to the minds of any one." It is the eloquence of description of what could be in heaven.**

In the Qur'an it is mentioned that there will be rivers of pure milk and Honey flowing in there, also there will be all kinds of fruits and food. There will be the top or the highest level of happiness any one could even think of, what ever you may wish you will get it. The wishes in the mind of the dwellers of the heavens will not be mean or demeaning as the people of this world's are.

They will live the life of luxury which could not even been thought of. Also, there are people of different level in heavens. They all deserve where they are placed in by the blessings of Allah. Any way we should not dwell too much about this , we should be working hard, ask and pray God for His blessings so that we may reach here in any level at all preferably we should work very hard and seek the highest level.

HELL:

God have made the proper places for the people who deserve those places. As heaven and its blessings was made for the believers and pious persons for the non believers and wrong doers the followers of Satan and his wrong advises.

Hell is the place for criminals and wrong doers. Those proud non-believers are destined to be there. The tyrants and killers and rapists and all the mischievous will be thrown in there. Those people who have given their own families, relatives, neighbors and their societies pain, shame and who never did any good deeds in their life, will belong in there.

The real unlucky or unfortunate ones are those who will not be able to make or cross it, and they will fall in the deep sea of ....
Hell Fire. Those are the tyrants who did not believe in God and

His oneness, and who killed others relentlessly and without a trace of remorse or mercy, or kindness to others. They are the ones who took pleasure in meeting atrocities and pain on others. Those are the ones who never gave charity, never did a good thing in their life and never spoke the truth. They are the ones who followed the lure and misguidance of Satan (Shaitan), who would himself leave them in their misery denouncing them. And who himself would be worrying about his own fate of sufferings eternal hell.

Hell also is made of stages or classes. It depends also on the severity of their crimes. People and rocks are the fuel of Hell fire. Women of no virtue and who brought shame on them-selves and their family are among those who are destined here. This is why in our lifetime we should do as much as we can to avoid being in this terrible place. God is just and merciful, He gave us all the chances and choices to avoid being thrown in this place, so we should have thanked Him and availed the opportunity in our lifetime to avoid being put in this dreadful situation.

AL SIRAT (THE PATH TO HEAVEN):

It is the only way or path which connects between the gathering place (Al Mahshar), where every one will be gathered after resurrection and heaven, on the Judgment day. It will be a bridge over hell. On that day everyone will be treading on this path, and will be assigned their proper and deserved places – in Heaven or hell. And this path of virtuous or the straight path is mentioned in the Qur'an:

"Guide us on the straight path, The path of those whom You have favoured, Not of those who have incurred Your wrath, Nor of those who have gone astray." (Al Fatiha)

Judgment day could be the longest day for humans. Because it is mentioned in the Qur'an:

"Indeed a day at your God's will be a thousand years of your count."

And to reach the heavens and enjoy what will be in it, everyone has to tread the virtuous path or the straight way which may have been made - to pass over hell. It may be like a bridge. It is a bridge not on the river "nile". But it will be a bridge of faith on the oceans of fire, Hell fire. All people and every one have to pass this path to arrive to the end of it to arrive heavens which is at the end of this path. Only the lucky and fortunate ones will be able, to pass or cross this straight path with the permission and blessings of God. The unlucky and unfortunate ones who did not believe in God and also in His oneness will never make it. From this path or before entering it they will be collected and thrown into hell by the guardians and servers who will catch the unlucky ones and throw or herded them in to hell.

People will be able to cross this path with the forgiveness or pardon from God, and enter heavens with His blessings, and take their right place through their right deeds.

HOW LONG THIS PATH? (ALSIRAT):

Too long is a simple answer. What is too long? It is any body's guess. It could be tens or hundreds or thousands of miles long. (Do not ask if it is statue miles or nautical miles - makes no difference then!).

The righteous path is described by Prophet *Mohammad* (peace be upon him)as sharper than the edge of a blade and thinner than the hair.

How people will cross it and how long it will take to do that, depends on our deeds in this world. Good deeds will certainly help speed up crossing over to the other end.

According to the sayings of the Prophet - some people will pass it like the lightning or speed of light. How this happens no one knows, because all things will be of different values and measures there, then what we humans calculate or expect in this world. Because all the worldly theories and calculations over there does not apply.

These are the chosen ones of Allah the Great, who would pass the path with such a lighting speed. They are the Messengers and Prophets of God, their true companions, the righteous and God fearing people whose life style was clean and spotless. They worshipped God, prayed for his blessings and did not indulge in selfishness and wrong or evil doings. They did not hurt their fellow human beings or any one for that matter, and they earned the love and blessing of Allah . Simply put: they did good deels and performed what they were ordained to do of prayers and worships faithfully, and refrained completely from wrong doings.

The others - or the rest, each according to his sayings and deeds. Good people will pass as fast as can be, and others may run or walk the distance, and the last ones are those who would be crawling to get over to the other side. You can imagine then how long and how miserable this journey of crossing this path will be, without the righteousness or piety (Al Taqwa), or our righteous deed which will be the proper fuel for this trip. Do not worry about dying; because there is no death after the resurrection, it is the suffering for ever or the happiness for ever. The lucky ones are those who pass or cross this straight path - however long it may be or however long time it might take to do it to reach the end. Because at the end, it is a life of joy and happiness. It is the life of heavens and all its blessings.

End Notes

Now we know a lot about the religion of Islam and its highly glorified symbol The Holy Ka'abah and the divine and holy book, the Qur'an. And it's Messenger Prophet *Mohammad* (peace be upon him), and His Companions.

Islam is an open book religion and there is no any secrecy about it, about its teachings, about its messages. There are no secret sects-services or rituals. If any one or any body proclaims other wise then either they are ignorant about it or they may be false pretenders of Islam.

Like any religion or subject one book like this is not enough. But I hope this book will give as much knowledge and information as possible about the subjects therein to satisfy the readers and their curiosity, and the desire of knowledge about Islam.

Let me stress here an important note. Nothing we could write or do can be perfect. And what is written is according to the best of my knowledge and ability. There may be some errors or omissions which are unintentional, and that would be my fault. But what ever good and useful information is in there, it is by the blessings of God.

To know more about Islam there are several means and ways:

1. The most important one is the holy book the Qur'an, which includes most of its rules and regulation. It contains all the information required while living in this world. It is like a constitution made for all times and all people and can be used anytime.

2. The second most important thing after the Qur'an, are the books which contains the sayings and doings of the Messenger of Islam Prophet Mohammad (peace be upon him). In these books we find the explanation and elaboration of most things came in the Qur'an. For example the prayers are mentioned in

the Qur'an, but the Prophet showed us how and when we can offer these prayers- This includes all the other rituals which we do, following the example of the Prophet. His sayings and deeds were a practical explanation of what The Qur'an states.

3.   And the most easier way to know any thing which we could not understand - we solicit it also from well known honest and righteous people who are scholars of Islam and who are learned persons. They will explain any information required. And they do not keep back any information. The scholars are well known and respected people in any city or country. And we can learn from them. (And ask the people of the Qur'an if you did not know) Qur'an.

I hope what you read and find in this book will make you dear reader a knowledgeable person and a good Muslim who should know as much about this religion. And that it will help in the daily life routine and can offer the rituals and prayers with the sense of knowledge and the satisfaction of being a Muslim - And we should thank Allah for this great Honour.

Prophet *Mohammad* (peace be upon him) in his farewell speech which he made in Arafat during Hajj, emphasized to the Muslims that he is leaving two things for them that if they adhered to, they will not go stray or wrong. Those two things he explained, are the holy divine book the Qur'an, and to follow his teachings. These two scriptures are very important to follow. One consists of the constitutions, and the other the Prophet's deeds and sayings which explains practically how these laws and orders are to be followed and executed.

The End

ISBN 142511492-X